T0193217

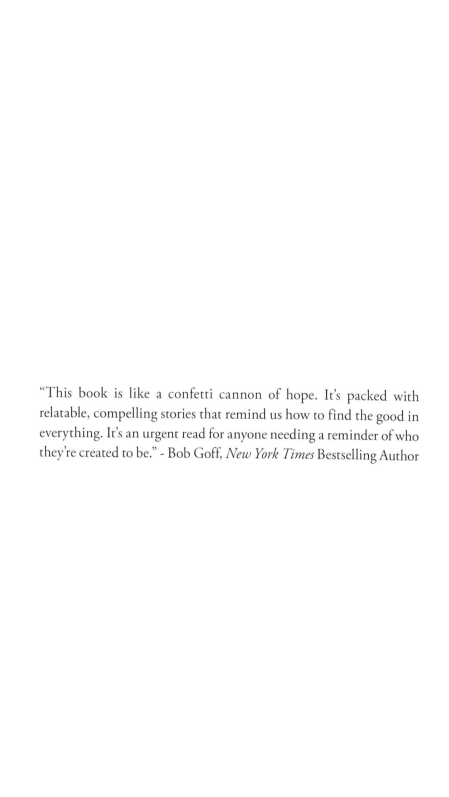

"This book is like a confetti cannon of hope. It's packed with relatable, compelling stories that remind us how to find the good in everything. It's an urgent read for anyone needing a reminder of who they're created to be." - Bob Goff, *New York Times* Bestselling Author

IT'S OK

FINDING PEACE IN UNEXPECTED PLACES

GRACE KHACHATURIAN

WESTBOW
PRESS®
A DIVISION OF THOMAS NELSON
& ZONDERVAN

WestBow Press books may be ordered through booksellers or by contacting:

WestBow Press
A Division of Thomas Nelson & Zondervan
1663 Liberty Drive
Bloomington, IN 47403
www.westbowpress.com
844-714-3454

ISBN: 978-1-6642-9584-1 (sc)
ISBN: 978-1-6642-9583-4 (hc)
ISBN: 978-1-6642-9585-8 (e)

Library of Congress Control Number: 2023905240

Print information available on the last page.

WestBow Press rev. date: 01/16/2024

Contents

PART 3 LIFE IS HOW YOU LOOK AT IT

To my family

PART 1
IN THE MIDST OF HOLY

Chapter 1

HOLY IN THE HEARTBREAK

IT WAS A WEDNESDAY NIGHT, AND I WAS SITTING ON MY BATHROOM floor. All the lights were off. Tears were streaming down my face, and my sweet little pup was pacing around me and trying to understand what these emotions were.

A breakup. A breakup with someone I had let my mind write a long story with, start to finish. So many pieces missing, so many pieces falling short of what I had hoped for. A story that had no basis to be imagined, built on a broken foundation of baseless expectations. Healing from our expectations of what we thought things would be is a dense and difficult feat.

We dated for a while, and things were great. I noticed some flags, but I let them slide. I figured I could deal with those things—or maybe things would change with time. Then, it became a long-distance relationship. I was absorbing the responsibility, effort, and financial aspect of the relationship. If I wanted to see him, it was up to me to get to where he was. It was up to me to crack open the piggy bank, find the vacation time, and prove that I was worthy of being wanted and seen. My deep brokenness was made so obvious. It's funny how exposing the story of a breakup can be. Reading this, it's easy to think, *Well, you shouldn't have been in that relationship in the first place.* Oftentimes, you don't see the reality of your situation until you're out of it.

I had gone to visit him a few times. We talked most nights to touch base. We were quickly approaching the next vacation days I had taken to go see him and looked at flights, but he hadn't mentioned that weekend. I had been asking about when I could fly in so that he would be able to pick me up. He kept avoiding the topic. And then, finally, on the phone, he told me that he wasn't sure I should come that weekend. If I didn't go that weekend, the next time I'd be able to visit would be two months later. Since he had no plans for coming to see me, this was the only way. As I began to ask more questions, he got off the phone. A few days of minimal, surface-level communication went by, and my heart was being pulled, squeezed, and torn in every direction. I was so confused about where we were. Were we still in a relationship?

We scheduled another call, and he shared the reasons he no longer wanted to be with me. I listened silently on the other side of the phone, absorbing every word and ounce of explanation. I asked for a phone call the next night. Until that next night, Wednesday night, I wrote out every question I could think of. My intent was closure. I needed it to walk away, move on, and heal. I believe an underlying intent was to convince him to go back to the relationship. I was trying, once again, to gather all the broken pieces and make it seem like things were OK. However, you can't hide a broken, sinking ship.

Nearing the end of the call, I knew it was the end. I did all I knew how to do to say a permanent goodbye that would allow me to not look back, and then I did something I did not expect. With open palms, I asked to pray for Him over the phone. I praised God for our time together, our difficult conversations, and all that was ahead of him. I believe this was the Spirit doing something He knew I couldn't without Him, but my fleshly side selfishly wanted his last experience with me to be one of honor and class.

Prior to the phone call, I had made up my mind that I would

only say things that I would hope someone would say to one of my brothers during such a difficult conversation. And shortly after we said amen, his dying phone caused us to arrive at the final, rushed goodbye. We've never spoken again.

Sharing about a breakup reveals your side of it. I had such a desire to be loved that I was willing to give up who I was to become who someone wanted me to be. Piece by piece, I was willing and ready to change. I was changing. This strong, confident version of who I was faded as my desire for affection from another broken person grew. As this desire grew, my expectations of him grew. And because my expectations of him were that of a savior, I was always left disappointed. Throughout the relationship, I prayed earnestly, filling pages of my prayer journal that he would "desire me" and want to "pursue me."

I had put all these hopes, prayers, and dreams of who I desired him to be on him without communicating these expectations. He wasn't anything like those hopes and dreams because he's human. I had put him in God's place. I had put him in my Savior's place, but because he, like me, is composed of flesh and blood, he couldn't meet those expectations. He wasn't my savior, and he never could be. No one could satisfy those expectations except the Savior Himself.

The night we broke up, I was so thankful for the conversations that led to the end, but it hurt so deeply. So deeply. Such sadness covered me. I found myself on my bathroom floor with tears streaming down my face. After some time passed, there on my apartment bathroom floor, the sweetest, faintest flare of hope came over me. I felt a peace like no other, just moments after a heartbreak. The words, "It's OK. It's going to be OK," were pressed into my spirit.

The weight of it all had been so heavy. All of a sudden, there was peace when it didn't make sense. All of a sudden, there was room to breathe, there was hope for all I didn't know to come, and there was space to heal and grow. All of a sudden, it was OK. The heartbreak excited me, but how? Why? That was not how it usually went.

Everything leading up to those moments was like riding a storm in a sinking ship. It was exhausting. I was holding it all together with a white-knuckled grip. I was constantly trying to pick up the pieces. I wanted everything to look intact—at least to the extent that I could convince others that things were going well.

Then I found a new hope. It looked much different than what I had begged for page by page and prayer by prayer throughout the relationship. It was nothing short of the peace that transcends all understanding. I found the holy in the heartbreak. It was not because of anything I had done; it was because of who God is. He brings peace when it doesn't make sense, and He opens our eyes and lets us find peace in unexpected places. Even our heaviest moments can be made holy.

This sweet new hope and the peace that didn't make sense didn't eliminate the hurt of it all. It empowered me to lean in and process the pain face-to-face, expediting the process. I still wanted to reach out. I still checked his social media here and there. I was still hoping for his comeback. I still had a whole lot of healing to do, but my eyes could rest on the One who is steady in the heartbreak. I could trust my Father that I was being saved from something and saved for someone.

Man, I'm sure God just aches with us in the hurt, but I bet He loves enabling us to process pain with His peace and holy hope in the moments we least expect it. He is most careful with you. He sees the big picture of life and knows what's good and best. He knows it's going to be OK.

MOZIE'S LITTLE RED BALL

Sometimes I think hurting comes with saving. There can be collateral pain when God changes our situations for our good. I believe God's intent is to save us from and for things. He wants to save us from ourselves and our own desires in order to change our situations, and

He wants to save us for the good and best that are coming. He knew how deeply that breakup would hurt me, but He knew that saving me from that relationship was worth the hurt it would bring. He knew it would stir up things in me that would allow His reflection to be a little clearer in me. God, the Author of all creation, has the power to make every single experience in life a process of refinement. When we lean in and trust His purpose for every big, small, and in-between experience, we enable Him to make us a little bit more like His Son.

During the relationship, I had been so consumed by what I wished it to be. It was as if I believed that's how things were. Things seemed good because of my skewed view of reality. It seemed deceivingly desirable, but the destruction was disguised in my desires. If only we could see the destruction some of our desires cause. It's easy to lose track of what things really are when it's the reality we're living in. We throw on those rose-colored glasses and become consumed with how we wished things were. We begin to believe that's how things really are—or we justify why they aren't that way.

My sweet little six-pound pup, Mozie—made up of fluff, spunk, and sweetness—loves exploring. She's got a nose like no other dog I've ever known. Her nose is her guide. One apartment complex I lived in had a clubhouse with fun amenities, including a community room, a gym, a study area, and a movie room. Mozie has always followed her guide well. One evening, while she was taking me on a tour through the clubhouse, she found a little red ball of chocolate under a chair. Of course, intrigued, she pulled it out and studied it closely. She put the little red ball in her mouth and trotted along on her tour.

I was mindlessly following her, stopping and starting, and we covered an impressively little amount of ground despite the time. Her proud prance caught my attention enough to know that she had something. I let her keep touring for a bit with her proud prance, but then I decided to lean down and check out what she had. When she turned away from me, I knew she had something she planned to keep—or eat. She was on her way to a place where she could enjoy her find, and she was afraid I would take away the little red ball she wanted. I swooped her up in my arms to get a closer look, afraid that what she had could be harmful to her. As I pried open her mouth, I saw the slightly eroded little red ball of chocolate that had inspired her proud prance. In my arms, she was doing all she could to squirm away from me and protect her little red ball.

Mozie knew I wouldn't approve of her discovery, and she was trying to keep me from taking it. Unfortunately for her, she had judged the situation well. I set her on the ground and took away the little red ball. I'm sure how tightly I was holding her was not comfortable and maybe even hurt a little bit, but I knew I needed to get it out of her mouth and throw it away. She looked at me with her big puppy eyes and begged for it. She didn't forget it for the rest of the night. She would randomly run up to me and check if I had changed my mind, hoping that I would return what she desired. Eventually, of course, she decided she would give it up and trust that I knew what was best.

Little did she know that what she desired so deeply could have been so destructive to her. She was unaware of what chocolate could do to her. Her little red ball seemed so good, deceivingly desirable, yet the destruction was disguised in her desire. She was afraid that I would take it away from her, but I knew that protecting her from that was worth the disappointment she'd experience. All I wanted to do was protect her from something that I knew would hurt her; sometimes, hurting comes with the saving.

It's funny how much I could relate to sweet little Mozie. It makes me wonder how much we do what Mozie did to God. We're making our way through life with our proud prancing, protecting what we've got from Him and afraid He will take it away. He's aware of what we have—even when we keep it from Him. What He takes away, He takes away because He knows something destructive is disguised in our desires. Down the road, we will eventually let go of our disappointments and the things we wanted to hold onto and see all He was saving us from.

When we decide to trust and believe He is most careful with us and is protecting us from all that could harm us, we will begin to find peace in those unexpected places. Maybe we'll begin to find that He's protecting us from something.

ONE DEGREE

Thank goodness God is in the business of saving because if I was left up to my own plan, a lot of damage would be done. Most people likely wouldn't go after something if they knew it would cause damage. Sometimes we just don't know; in fact, most of the time, we just don't know. God's love steps in, sweeps us off our feet, and protects us from the destruction He sees down the line.

When we're the ones calling the shots, it's all too easy to wander off the intended route. Imagine if I let Mozie have one little red ball of chocolate a week. It may seem like one tiny treat a week, but that would end up being a ton of poison in her system. Having one treat like a little red ball of chocolate can lead us to be one degree off. One time turns into a few times, which turns into a couple more. The number of times it occurs begins to add up, and before we know it, it's a habit. One degree could become a continuous decision we allow as we become desensitized, and it could end up throwing us completely off course.

Let's look at it the way the one and only Christine Caine describes it. If a pilot was taking a flight from Chicago to Dallas and was one degree off their course, a slight course adjustment could probably fix the error. They would likely still end up in the same vicinity. However, if the flight was going from Chicago to Hong Kong, that one degree would have an enormous impact. I would imagine they would end up in an entirely different country—far from where they intended to be. If just one degree can make such a big difference, imagine how much of a difference any more could make?

Are we just one degree from who God created us to be? Or are we many more? Are we aligned with the path He has set before us—or have we wandered off a bit?

Between now and next week, that one degree probably would not be a big deal. We would most likely stay near the same path, but in five years, that one degree would totally change the course of our lives and who we have become and are becoming. We would find ourselves on a path we had trampled down ourselves and in a place we never intended to be. It all began by being off by just one degree. It reveals the power of just one degree. What's causing that slight deviation in your life? One degree can change everything. Let's make the course adjustment before we find ourselves in a place we never intended to be.

Thank goodness we have a God who catches us on our "one-degree" decisions, whether that is a little red ball or a breakup. He loves us too much to let us stray off course, one decision at a time. He sees the destruction where we see desires, but He knows what's good. He will correct you in order to protect you. Hurting comes with the saving, but the holy meets us in the heartbreak. Hold on. It's OK.

Chapter 2

REST AT ROCK BOTTOM

I HAVE A DEEP FEAR OF BEING UNDERWATER.

At one point in time, I decided to become a PADI-certified scuba diver. I still chuckle at the thought of how I came to the conclusion to do that considering how uncomfortable I am in water. I quickly learned that scary and difficult moments call us to be fully present. The training began with a swim test that was way harder than I expected. In each class, we learned a number of required skills and had to successfully show our proficiency in them before progressing. Before advancing to more complicated skills, you had to demonstrate you could do the basics, and they would continuously build on each skill. Each skill is completely necessary for learning to breathe, function, and be underwater at various depths.

One of the dives landed on a late-October, snowy day in the Midwestern climate of Illinois. It was anything but a comfortable climate, and the visibility underwater was subpar to say the least. Naturally, that was the class I was required to successfully complete a number of skills that I, in particular, did not enjoy.

One of those skills was face mask removal, twenty-two feet underwater, in the darkness of an Illinois Lake in late October. Yeah, no thanks. I would have rather woken up to taking the ACT all day than do this one task that scared me more than anything. Yet there, twenty-two feet under, I was required to take off my mask, put it back on, and empty out all the water. The anxiety I had built around this skill was layered and thick. What if I breathed through my nose and got choked up underwater? What if I panicked and tried to swim to the surface? You can't just swim up from that depth underwater because you could damage your ears or lungs. What if I couldn't get the water out of my mask? I had so many questions and so much fear.

My family was getting certified together, and the class was made up of my people, which helped. As we were on our knees on the bottom of the Illinois lake, one by one, we were motioned to remove our masks. As I was motioned to remove my mask, I focused on taking in a big breath through my regulator (air source), and before thinking too long, I removed my mask. Barefaced and exposed, it was like I had dunked my face in all my fear and anxiety. Even there, there was air, and I had to choose whether I would calm myself enough to breathe.

I drew my focus to each breath. I was thinking about every breath just through my mouth and not my nose. I tend to breathe through my nose, which is obviously problematic for scuba diving. I took a breath through my regulator to know that, even there, there was still air to breathe. I sat there for a few moments, knowing that I could sit in the culmination of all my fear and anxiety and still breathe. I could just be. I could still find comfort there. I could still find rest. I could still find peace, right there on rock bottom. It was all OK.

What's so interesting about that moment was that my full focus was on our most instinctive habit: breathing. All I could focus on was each inhale and each exhale. There wasn't room for anything else—and that's exactly what I did.

Inhale.

"It's OK."

Exhale.

After a few breaths, I put my mask back on my face and tilted my head slightly up while pressing on the top of the mask and breathing out my nose as hard as I could to clear out the water. Then, after another breath with my mask emptied of all the water and my eyes tightly closed, I slowly opened my eyes to find I was OK. It was all OK. In the moments leading up to removing my mask, the instructor knew my fear and anxiety. He came face-to-face with me. Eye to eye. He wanted me to know he was right there. He could help me at any moment. He would save me. And when I opened my eyes, he was right there.

Face-to-face.

Eye to eye.

He was always there. It's the same with the Lord. When our knees hit rock bottom, He comes in close.

He comes face-to-face.

Eye to eye.

He wants you to know He's right there. He can help at any moment. He saves. When we open our eyes, He is right there. On rock bottom, every ounce of my attention was in that very moment. What a gift scary and challenging moments can be. Fear, discomfort, and intensity welcome us to be completely present to our most instinctive habits. Even in those moments, the Creator of the universe is always with us, in each and every breath. Tremendous growth happens in the places of discomfort. He's tending to the seeds He's growing in you, the qualities that can only be developed outside the perimeter of a comfort zone and the qualities He knows will be valuable in who He's created you to be. Maybe rock bottom is where we need to go to discover that we don't need our comfort zones to find peace and be OK.

He is paving the places of discomfort with supernatural peace that only He can provide. When we answer the call to be fully present, even at rock bottom, we'll find that it's OK. Even on rock bottom, there is peace. Even on rock bottom, there is rest. I may not find myself at the bottom of an Illinois lake too often (thankfully), but I'll practice the posture and presence that I learned there.

When life is good or difficult, you'll find me on my knees,

focusing on each breath. Sometimes being and breathing is our bravest and most persevering posture. In the midst of the heaviness, you'll find yourself able to sit in the culmination of all fear and anxiety and still breathe. Right here and right now needs us first and foremost, which disarms the pressure to be anywhere but in that moment—not a minute ahead and not a minute behind. Sitting in the discomfort allows us to carve new depths with each breath, expanding who we are and what we're capable of handling, and refining us to be a little bit more like our Savior.

Once we are steady with each breath, and we open our eyes, we'll find the water emptied and see our Savior face-to-face and eye to eye. Everything is OK. There is always air to breathe. So, whether you find yourself on your knees on the rock bottom of an Illinois lake or the middle of your kitchen floor, God has always been—and will always be—right there, paving the way for peace in unexpected places. Even there, on rock bottom, you'll find it's OK.

CORNER OF THE DOCK

One of my favorite places on this earth is called the Malibu Club. It's a sweet little Young Life camp tucked away in the Princess Louisa Inlet in British Columbia, Canada. The only way to get there is by boat or seaplane, and it is roughly sixty miles from any civilization. Every week of summer, hundreds of high school campers arrive at Malibu by boat. They usually come with a group of their peers, and a few leaders usually being college students who they have grown relationships with back home. Throughout the week, campers get to do a range of camp-wide activities, competitions, a ropes course, zip line canopy tour, huge tree swing, sailing, kayaking to a waterfall, doing all sorts of water sports, and so much more. Every night, campers go to something called club. At club, all the campers and leaders sing well-known pop songs by artists we all know. Then, they play some sort of wacky game. To round out club, a speaker comes up onto the stage and shares the message of Jesus, little by little, each night. Following club, the campers and leaders go back to their cabins to talk about their thoughts on club. Camp is intentionally structured to encourage and support relationships to grow with the people campers came with because they're the same people they will go home with.

I had the honor of serving at the Malibu Club over the span of a couple summers in various roles. One summer, I worked on the outer dock, which was about half a mile from camp. I was the sailing and kayak instructor. During the day, tons of campers came together to ride the banana boat or sail.

On one of the first days of camp, the dock was full of campers. They were hanging out with different groups of people they came with. Different clumps of people lined the dock. On the far-right side of the dock, a girl was sitting alone. Her toes were brushing the top of the water with each wave. She had a great view. The panorama of mountains towered over the water. She sat there for a long time that day, and then she came back the next day—and the next day. I began to catch on.

Every afternoon, I'd look to the corner of the dock and see her, by herself, feet brushing the top of the waves. I decided to go sit with her. I went and hung my legs over the edge like hers, and I introduced myself. We will call her Allie. At first, Allie didn't have much to say. There was a lot of space for silence. I didn't mind. I just sat there enjoying the view too. The next day, she came back, and I took my place next to her. Each day, she shared a bit more. One afternoon, she shared why she was sitting alone. She didn't know why she was there, and she didn't want to be there. Her leaders had brought her. She didn't want to go home either. Allie didn't have a safe place. She felt like she didn't fit in there or where she came from. She questioned where she belonged and why she was there. She shared the brokenness she had left and the brokenness she would return to. She didn't want to stay, and she didn't want to go back.

Everything seemed just heavy and hard at the ripe age of

13

fourteen. As time passed, I discovered who Allie's leader was, and she began to join our corner-of-the-dock conversations. We began to talk through the heavy and hard together. We began to create a space Allie had not yet had: a place of safety. A space where it was all OK. A space that could make room for hope in her heart. Even in the heavy and hard, there was hope, there was purpose, there was peace, and there was rest. She found an invitation to a life with Jesus on the corner of the dock, but she also found a place where she belonged. Regardless of the rock bottom she was facing, she was noticed, seen, heard, and loved. She was worthy of taking up space.

All it took to create a space for rest to be found on rock bottom was eyes that noticed someone in the corner. Allie left that dock a few days later and returned to face her reality. This time, she came back with a new space in her heart for hope. Allie isn't the only one who faces rock bottom after rock bottom. She isn't the only one searching for her place and part in this world. Whether you're in a similar boat to Allie or feeling like you're doing just fine, you have an opportunity every day. You have an opportunity to notice those in the corners of our lives. We all have an opportunity to notice and go sit next to those people and remind them of the hope ahead and their part and place in this world. We get to bring the good news. No matter what rock bottom they're facing, rest can be found in the thick of it.

I left that sweet and sacred dock a few weeks after Allie, but I still practice the posture I found there on the corner of the dock. I gained a new perspective and ability to notice those in the corner. My eyes began to look more and more to the outskirts, to the corners, to those who sit by themselves. What if we dared to go to other people's rock bottoms and meet them there so they would know they're not alone. Who you notice and where you notice them are not accidents. Maybe God is opening your eyes to this person at just the moment they need it most. Our simple obedience to go sit next to those in the corners could change everything—from their faith, their future, and their forever.

Let's notice those who occupy the corners of life, whether that is the corner of your workplace, classroom, or kitchen table. God loves using people to remind those hurting of His rest, holiness, and hope to be found in the heavy and hard. Maybe your presence, and the space you create, will help them find peace in unexpected places and realize, even at rock bottom, there is rest. Even at rock bottom, it's OK.

NEIGHBOR MIKE

One Saturday night, I was blow-drying my hair. All of a sudden, I heard a noise. It took me two seconds to turn to my left and see the supply line to my toilet flailing with water shooting out of it. At first, I had no idea what was happening. I had no idea what a toilet supply line was before that experience. And since I had no idea what the hose-looking thing was, I had no idea why it was shooting water or how to stop it. I had no idea where the main water shutoff valve was.

I immediately called my dad. He knew exactly the problem and how to stop the water. I listened to every word he said. He told me to turn the valve on the wall the supply line was attached to. I kept turning the valve. I tried both directions. I turned the rusted valve hard enough to puncture my hands, yet nothing was happening. My bathroom was quickly flooding.

Within minutes, the water was ankle deep—and it was still rushing out. After realizing the only solution we knew of, outside of the main water shutoff valve, was not working, I decided I needed help. I needed to get someone. But who? I couldn't think of anyone to call. It was such a heart-wrenching, hollow feeling.

At ten forty-five on a Saturday night, I picked up my sweet pup, Mozie, and with the water still shooting out of the supply line, I ran as fast as I could to my neighbor's house. I had seen him in passing with a young son. I rang the doorbell, and after a few slow moments, the door opened. From my dripping wet shirt and distressed spirit, he could tell I needed help. I quickly introduced myself and told him my house was flooding and I needed help.

Neighbor Mike told me he couldn't leave his sleeping toddler. He told me he would call the emergency maintenance line. I ran to the next neighbor, Neighbor Tom, and after explaining the situation again, he ran back with me to my flooding apartment. Without any hesitation, he walked through the deepening waters—straight to the gushing supply line. After a few more moments of intensely handling the valve, the water slowed.

Neighbor Tom said he couldn't believe it stopped because the valve seemed completely unattached and unresponsive. The water slowed, but the standing water remained. It was deep and had seeped into the surrounding rooms. Neighbor Tom headed home because the water was leaking through to his garage.

I ran back to Neighbor Mike's house to check if he had heard from emergency maintenance. He walked out of his garage with a stack of towels that was tall enough to cover the top of his head. Then, another neighbor, Neighbor Josh, noticed the commotion and asked how he could help. He quickly came out of his garage with another towering stack of towels.

Neighbor Mike rolled out his shop-vac. Neighbor Josh carried the shop-vac while I took the towels, and he started vacuuming up all the water. Eight gallons of water filled the tank in a couple minutes, and it seemed like it hadn't made the slightest dent.

After a good twenty minutes, Neighbor Josh went home to continue his birthday celebrations with his little boy. I continued to try to vacuum up all the water I could. I finally heard back from emergency maintenance.

The next morning, the emergency maintenance and a plumber arrived. After thorough inspections, both kept questioning how the water had stopped. The valve was completely broken. Neither of them knew where the main water shutoff valve was, and they said all there was left to do was let the apartment flood. A miracle had saved my safe space.

All I could see in those initial moments was the rushing water flooding my home. It was crowding out my hope and faith. Once I couldn't get the source to stop the problem, I ran to someone who I thought could. I was desperate for any help. Neighbor Mike was the first person I ran to, and he jumped into action in the ways he could. Neighbor Mike, Neighbor Tom, and Neighbor Josh all helped in the ways they could.

What if we did that where we saw need? What if we jumped into action in the ways we could? Those people who came running into my mess shifted my focus from the problem that was crowding out my faith to the people who showed up. Strangers ran to my rescue and showed me the true meaning of the word *neighbor*. Strangers rushed to help me and walked right into the mess without considering what it would cost them. What if, when we saw need, we ran to the rescue in all the ways we could? Strangers can take care of strangers, and they will soon become neighbors and friends. My sweet neighbors saw the urgency of my situation. Their mere presence turned my attention from the problem to the people.

Because of that experience, Neighbor Mike and I became friends. He texted me one night and asked about my faith. He shared his desperate need for the power of prayer over his situation. He was on the verge of losing custody of his young son, and he needed everyone in his corner to plead to the Father on his behalf. And we did. We prayed earnestly for his situation. A couple weeks went by, and after a horrific trial, Neighbor Mike won. He got joint custody and traced every bit of it to the power of prayer. It's hard to know God's purpose behind situations, but He can use them to connect you to the people around you.

Maybe the people on the outside of our situations know how to navigate or stop the source of all the damage better than we do. Maybe they have a solution that we weren't aware of. Their presence can turn our focus from the problem to the people. I think that's God's hope. At rock bottom, He wants us to turn to the people around us.

Allow yourself to be accessible to help and saving by revealing the reality of your mess. Maybe it's not a matter of what happens to us; it's *who* happens to us. So, whether you're a Neighbor Mike or the one at rock bottom, run to help. In the midst of it all, you'll find your focus shifting from the problem to the people. Strangers, neighbors, family members, therapists, friends, teachers, and pastors can help us find peace in unexpected places. They can show us that we're not alone—even at rock bottom. Even at rock bottom, there is rest. Even at rock bottom, it's OK.

Chapter 3

HERE IS HOLY

AT THE MALIBU CLUB, I HAD THE OPPORTUNITY TO BE ON "BIRD poop patrol." On BPP, we got to take spray bottles and rags and scrub the bird poop off the dock. For some reason, there always seemed to be an abnormally large amount of really gross bird poop—like a whole lot. Being in an inlet of the ocean, the birds were often seagulls.

When I heard "BPP," I wasn't exactly thrilled. I would wiggle my hands into the blue latex gloves, grab the orange cleaning spray and my stained, fraying rag, and get down on my hands and knees to put a little elbow grease into each scrub. It was pretty gross, but there was something so sweet about the quietness, evident progress, and light yet satisfying labor. It was a place no one really wanted to be, but it was a place that not many got to be. It was a place where you would see the fruits of your own labor with each scrub. It was a place where it was just you, a panorama of mountains, a spray bottle, a rag, and waves lightly swaying the worn dock. At times, it was easy to think the labor was pointless since the dock would need to be cleaned again within the hour, but I began to love BPP because it was a time of stillness and evidence of a holy presence.

Bird poop patrol taught me that here is holy. It was the place and dwelling of a powerful, gentle presence. I found unexpected peace in the place no one wanted to be. In the place no one wanted to be, I realized that right here is holy—if we choose to notice and acknowledge it. Even in the place no one wanted to be, it was OK. It was all OK.

One day, during bird poop patrol, I was thinking about heaven. A precious image came to my mind. I was on a porch, overlooking my front yard, and it was lined with a chipped and worn picket fence. The yard was overgrown and thick with tall weeds. A man dressed in white was cutting down the thick brush and pulling weeds. He was dripping sweat, and his brown hair was messy and soaked. It was Jesus. He was clearing the way of everything that stood between Him and me. He was preparing a place for me.

Getting to scrub docks of bird poop was one of the greatest honors I will ever have. It was the dock that could give kids a glimpse of the place Jesus is preparing for them. It was the dock that maybe kids would witness Jesus dripping sweat, cleaning out everything in the way between Him and them. It was the dock where maybe kids would meet Jesus for the first time. It was the dock that maybe kids would find for the first time, that here, right here, is holy. What an honor it was to prepare a place for a glimpse of what's to come—a glimpse of heaven.

Jesus is most present in the places no one wants to be. Those are the holy places filled with His gentle whispers and ground-trembling power. Those are the places where we get a glimpse of the hope that's coming. Those are the places we get a glimpse of the care He is putting into the place He is preparing for us. Those are the places we find unexpected peace and find that here—no matter where that is—is holy.

Let's run to the places no one would choose to be. Those are the places that will show you that here is holy. Those are the very places you'll find peace in unexpected places. Whether that's on bird poop patrol or doing laundry, you'll find Him there, dripping sweat and cutting down everything standing between you and Him because here is holy.

SIXTY-NINE-CENT CAN OF SPAGHETTI

On April 25, 2017, I learned the power of a sixty-nine-cent can of spaghetti. The holy is often found in people.

My brother Benjamin and I were studying abroad for the semester in Dunedin, New Zealand. When we could, we would travel throughout the country to explore. On April 25, 2017, we were at the airport in Auckland, New Zealand, and the only food we had was a sixty-nine-cent can of spaghetti. To say we were hungry was an understatement. We had planned all day to just grab dinner at the airport, but they didn't have food at the Auckland airport past certain hours. Who knew?

Benjamin wasn't discouraged by that in the slightest bit. He saw it as a challenge to use what he had. While waiting at the gate, he used his wallet-sized letter opener to open his sixty-nine-cent can of spaghetti. He managed to poke a few holes to form a larger hole that was the size of a quarter. As he was focused on piercing his can, the family sitting across from us was incredibly amused. They would look at his hands and back at each other over and over, trying to confirm what they were seeing.

After a few more minutes of unsuccessfully attempting to make the hole bigger, Benjamin just began to slurp the spaghetti through the quarter-sized hole. After a couple minutes, I jumped in on the slurping action, trying to get as many noodles as I could. Finally, I guess we had moved from an amusing sight to just embarrassing.

The mom sitting across from us said, "Can I do something nice for you?" She explained that her friend had just given her a bag of fresh avocados and limes, and she handed one of each to us. This led to more conversation, which ended with an exchange of contacts and an invitation to tea at their home once we landed.

We took them up on tea, and we ended up becoming quite close with that family. We stayed with them multiple times, and we even introduced the rest of our family when they arrived in New Zealand. They opened their homes and lives to two people slurping noodles out of a sixty-nine-cent can of spaghetti. At first, they gave what they had, and then they gave all they had to offer: home-cooked meals, warm beds, generous hospitality, and two seats at their kitchen table. The mom would even fill grocery bags with everything she had in her garden for us every time we left from a visit.

The mundane, ordinary, desperately amusing, and even embarrassing moments may just be making space for the holy and the sweet gifts from God that often come in the form of people. People notice need, and they act on it. Maybe here, no matter where we are, is holy because of the people.

The holy we found in this family began over a rather hopeless letter opener's attempt at a sixty-nine-cent can of spaghetti and the eyes that took the time to notice, share a little chuckle, and decide to love the people in front of them. God provides and cares for us in simple and meticulous ways.

Let's take the time to notice those around us. Let's be the people who act when there is a need. Let's be the people who allow others to see that it's OK. Let's be the people who allow others to see the peace in unexpected places. Let's be the people who allow others to see that here is holy because of the people. Let's be those people. Who knows? It may all begin over a sixty-nine-cent can of spaghetti.

STUCK WITH STRANGERS

I was flying from Charlotte to Chicago and Chicago to Bloomington—and just about everything went wrong in the last leg of the flight. It was spring, and it was a late rainy evening in Bloomington. I was on the last flight there for the night. My seat was next to an off-duty pilot who often did this route to Bloomington. There was very minor turbulence throughout the flight, and every once in a while, the off-duty pilot would check his iPad to look at something about the plane and flight status.

When we were about to land in Bloomington, the pilot announced on the PA system that we were waiting for our turn to land. After we circled the Bloomington runway several times, it was finally our turn. As we were about to touch down, a wave of relief came over me. It had been such a long weekend and travel day.

All of a sudden, we began to ascend again. The off-duty pilot whipped out his iPad and started studying something I couldn't understand.

The pilot came on the PA system and said, "Sorry, folks. I'll have to try that landing again." The pilot circled around, and we were finally about to touch down. A wave of relief came over me. All of a sudden, we began to ascend again.

The off-duty pilot looked at his iPad and said, "Yep, we're not landing here tonight."

The pilot came over the PA and said, "Sorry, folks. We're having a hard time seeing the runway tonight, and we're going to head back to Chicago."

I thought, *This is a joke, right?* I asked the off-duty pilot, and he said, "Yep, we're going back to Chicago."

During the flight, I was brainstorming options for getting home, which was just sixty minutes from Bloomington. I could rent a car in Chicago and drive home, which was only two hours, or I could wait for the rescheduled flight.

We arrived in Chicago around midnight. After deplaning, all the passengers were waiting at the gate for another attempt after visibility improved. The flight crew was going to try to make the trip back that same evening. We were told we would board again in forty-five minutes. After three forty-five-minute delays, they canceled the flight at close to three in the morning. All the passengers stood in line to rebook their flights and claim a hotel stay covered by the airline. Most of us chose the next option at six thirty in the morning.

Little by little, the passengers trickled out. Many were looking for a shuttle to get to the hotel or standing inside a little vestibule near the arrivals pick-up street. Shuttle after shuttle arrived, and the number of passengers was dwindling. It was down to about six of us. I guess we had all chosen the same hotel, which was clearly the wrong pick. We shared a few words here and there. When the shuttle pulled up, we all got in.

During the drive, we began to process the eventful evening together. The range of emotions ranged from frustration to anger to sadness to annoyance. We had all felt such similar things throughout the experience and internalized them all. One person shared how they felt about it, and it opened the door to everyone else identifying the emotions they felt. There was space for all that was felt, and no matter what someone said, at least one other person could relate.

We began to share the "at leasts." "At least, we got rebooked." "At least they covered our hotels." Together, we were able to bring light to the blessings that we hadn't noticed before. It is amazing how vulnerability invites vulnerability—even when it's processing a stressful experience with complete strangers.

I think God intended us to lean on each other to process what we're holding in, share each other's burdens, and delight in where each other's blessings were found. When we process things, especially with other people, we find peace in unexpected places—even where we didn't see any space for peace before.

After processing the heavy, we are able to find the holy because there is holy in the heavy. There is power in processing. It took the voices of others to help me see the good where I hadn't before. Vulnerability invites vulnerability. You may be the first to offer the invitation, but together, you'll find peace in unexpected places and realize that even here is holy. Even here, it's OK.

$Chapter 4$

LIFE LESSONS AT THE SALAD BAR

WHEN YOU GO TO A SALAD BAR, IT'S STOCKED WITH ALL THE options: veggies, fancy little salads, and an array of cheeses and proteins. It can be a little overwhelming with so much to choose from.

As I was making my way through the salad bar, there was a line on each side. Each side had its own variety of options. As I was going through, I had my eye on the other side the whole time. I really just wanted all the options that were over there. I was discontent with everything that was right in front of me because I was so consumed with all that was out of reach.

How often do we do the same thing in life that we do at the salad bar? We see all we don't have. We see all we aren't. We see all everyone else has and all they are. As we do that, we're conditioning our eyes to get in the routine of seeing life from that lens. We miss all that's right in front of us because we're so consumed by all that's out of reach. Let's not miss what's right in front of us. If you're looking for all that's missing, you'll find it. Try looking beneath your nose at all that's in front of you. There's good there too. Let's look for it.

It's funny that everybody else in the salad bar line could have had a similar mindset. Their eyes were on all they couldn't reach and didn't have, but all their eyes were on something different. One person may think the chicken salad looks great. One person may think the homemade honey mustard is all they need to have the perfect salad. Everyone believes their salad needs something different to be complete, a certain combination they think will satisfy. As we progress down the salad bar line, what was once in reach will no longer be in reach. With each step, new things come, and all the things that were once right in front of us go. What we once overlooked because it wasn't what we wanted at the time may be something we later hope for but is out of reach. It's the same in life as it is at the salad bar. Let's not miss what's right in front of us at this moment. It's good stuff, and it may soon be out of reach.

This is awfully similar to the way you and I think. Once we get this combination of things, we'll be satisfied. Whether that is a salad bar or a day-to-day approach. We are conditioning our eyes to always be looking for what we don't have, and we are convincing ourselves that we'll be satisfied once we get them.

As we practice this mindset, we are developing it as a routine. Our habits will eventually become subconscious. Who knew we had so much to learn from a salad bar? We have to be intentional in protecting our minds from infrequent thought processes that begin to take root and breed discontentment. Every thought process is rewiring our minds to function in some way. It can be looking at all that we don't have, all that's out of reach, or all that we do have.

Maybe the day-to-day things were meant to teach us more. Maybe you'll see a salad bar a little differently from here on out. Let's take great care and intention in what we're conditioning our eyes to see. Take inventory of all that is in reach—all that we do have—and condition our eyes not to miss the good that is right in front of us. When we recognize all we *do* have, little by little, we'll find gratitude and peace in unexpected places. We'll find right here is overflowing with more than enough and blessing upon blessing.

THE MORE WE DRINK,
THE LIGHTER THE LOAD

Every night, right before bed, I fill up an obnoxiously large water bottle that tops off at a gallon. Along the side of the gray, gradient bottle, it has benchmark goals: "7:00: Good morning," "9:00: Hydrate yourself," and so on. When I wake up, I begin sipping away to set the pace to reach the goal of a gallon by the end of the day. I don't reach my goal every day. One reason to drink as I go is how heavy the bottle is if I don't. A gallon of water is not light. As I consume the water throughout the day, it becomes lighter and lighter. I think it's the same way in life.

The more good stuff we consume, the more good stuff we find. If we've conditioned our eyes to see all the negatives, we're conditioning our minds to search for the negatives. Whether it is circumstances or people, there are plenty of Negative Nancies and Debbie Downers. Unfortunately, it's easy to condition our eyes to see everything that inconveniences us or causes any sort of discomfort or frustration. It's easy to always look for the things that go wrong. Carrying loads that never get lighter is a heavy way to live.

Minds conditioned to see the negative are usually more reactive to life. They let life throw what it will, and they wince at the pain of it. We all do this throughout our lives. Try to be on the flip side and seek and find the good everywhere. Instead of letting life happen to us, let's happen to life. If we consume what's good, we will see what's good. And then we'll find—no matter the weight of life—the more good we consume, the lighter the load. We'll condition our eyes to see the good in everything, all the time.

This idea also applies to our faith. The more we drink of the Living Water, the lighter the weight of the world becomes. When we are filled with what's good, the weight of the world seems to affect us less and less. We can look to Jesus as the perfect example for this. Despite all the things life threw at Him—from dishonor to death itself—He remained steady. His eyes were conditioned to remain steady on His purpose, unshaken by His circumstances. Life didn't happen to Him; He happened to life. Whether falling asleep, on the mountainside or on the cross, He was always talking to His Father. Jesus was always consuming what's good: the truth of His Father. Since He consumed what's good, His load was light. His eyes were conditioned to see the holy in the heartbreak, the good in every moment, and peace in the most unexpected places. Even His worst days would someday be deemed good.

Just as I do with my obnoxiously large water bottle, let's fill up on all that sustains and satisfies. From our first morning moments and throughout the day, let's keep consuming the good. The more we drink, the lighter our loads will be. We must continually condition our eyes. The more good we consume, the more good we'll see—and the more peace we'll find in unexpected places.

The Purpose of a Rain Jacket

Put on your rain jacket. If every negative thought that trickles through our minds was a raindrop, we'd likely be soaked in the first hour of our day. Everything that happens to us that is outside of how we thought things would go becomes a breach in the day's blueprint. It becomes an offense that we pick up and carry. If our minds are conditioned to notice all the things happening *to* us, we'll notice one offense at a time, which will drench us in negativity. When we look for the negative, we will find the negative. If all the negativity were raindrops, you'd be pretty sopping wet, uncomfortable, and soggy. It would be a heavy load to bear.

I think faith is like a rain jacket. When we sit with our heavenly Father in the first moments of the day, it's as if we are putting on our rain jackets. After that, every drop of negativity and every offense rolls right off. Nothing sticks or stains. You may begin to not even notice or feel the drops as they come. Putting on your rain jacket conditions your mind in faith over fear, faith in our Father, and no fear of the offenses to come. We'll find we're steady and secure in His protection as we consume His truth.

It takes too much energy to walk around noticing and carrying the weight of every drop of negativity. There is no need to get soaked. Before we consider the scattered showers forming and the day ahead, let's sit with our heavenly Father and put on our rain jackets. When we do, we'll find peace in the most unexpected places as the offenses roll right off. Even in the most severe storms, it's OK. Put on your rain jacket.

We have so much to learn in our day-to-day lives. Whether it is a salad bar, a water bottle, or a rain jacket, let's condition our minds with care and intention and take inventory of all that we are and the blessings upon blessings that are right in front of us. Fill up on all that's trustworthy and true and drink of it often. The more you drink of the Living Water, the lighter all the rest becomes. Throw on that rain jacket and watch the offenses roll right off. Storms have nothing on eyes that are conditioned to seek and find peace in unexpected places. It's time to happen to life rather than letting life happen to us because—no matter what—it's OK.

Chapter 5

THE MIX-UP

As you know, I have a six-pound ball of fluff, cuteness, and spunk that I refer to as my sweet pup, little bear, and officially Mozie Bear (Moe-zee). She has about a four-inch clearance from the ground, big paws she tries to use like hands, and the sweetest, most opinionated personality. A few weeks after moving to a new state on my own, the pandemic hit—and then little 1.8-pound Mozie Bear came home.

She quickly became my little shadow. It was just her and me. We knew each other best. Our routines, our mannerisms, our favorite places to be, we were two peas in a pod. She went with me everywhere. I was that person. I just stuck her in my tote bag, and we did every single thing together. We just love being with each other. Whether it's sharing a pillow for "night night," sitting outside the bathroom while I shower, sitting like a little teddy bear on the porch and watching the world go by, shopping, or road tripping, we're always with each other. She's a joy and delight, and she helps me keep life in balance. She reminds me of all the little things that matter and last and the joy in simplicity. For two years, it was just us. Anywhere we are together, we're safe and home.

However, she is still a dog. Oftentimes, she feels more like my companion, but she does have the typical puppy tendencies. Sometimes she mixes up Mama's carpet for the grass, Mama's shoes for her toys, and Mama's food for her own. I know it can be confusing, but sometimes the mix-ups can spark a good bit of frustration. Her fluff, cuddly tendencies, and natural puppy eyes have not made discipline my strong suit—and she knows it. I hate to admit it, but these puppy tendencies make it easy to mix up the burdens for the blessings.

I sometimes find myself seeing my sweet little bear as a hassle, an inconvenience, or a burden. It breaks my heart to recognize that perspective of the sweetest pup that has been such a blessing and saving grace in so many moments. I'm getting teary just writing this. She's been the one to meet me on the bathroom floor or kitchen floor when life is just too difficult to stand. She is the only one that's seen the heavy and hard before I could find the holy. She has seen me in the thick of heartbreak and some of life's lowest lows. She's seen me in those dark, lonely spaces and curled up next to me, reminding me that I wasn't alone. She's been a source of comfort and safety when I was all alone. She's been a witness to the weakest and weariest side of me. What a gift!

Mozie Bear has shown me that all of creation points us to our Creator. She is a gift that constantly reminds me of the Giver. Her presence reminds me of the sweet and constant presence of God. He has also been with me in those dark, quiet spaces. For all of my days, it's always been my sweet Savior.

In the same way that Mozie Bear laid with me in the shadows, our heavenly Father does too. Years and years ago, I had a dream. I was in a huge room that was almost like a cathedral with tall, fancy ceilings and double doors. It was empty. There were no pews or people. The marble tiles were black and white. The center of the cathedral was lit, and pillars lined the perimeter. The front of the court had steps that led to the throne of Jesus. I was lying on my side on the floor with the top of my head barely illuminated by the light, and the rest of my body was covered by the shadows. I was near the steps to the throne. The One on the throne stepped down and lay there in the shadows next to me.

Mozie Bear reminds me of the relationships we have with our parents. People say, "I messed up, and my dad is going to kill me," or "I messed up, and I need to call my dad." My struggle with discipline has led me to lead and teach Mozie from a perspective of love. There is always room for grace in the mess-ups. When she does mess up, and I'm cleaning an accident or moping to get the message across to her, she runs up to me. She looks like she's trying to be held in grace. Instead of running away from me, she runs *to* me, which has been a neat way to look at God's love. What if we did this with our heavenly Father? "I messed up, and I need to call my dad." If I feel this way about my dog, imagine how God feels about His children that He sent His only Son to die for. There is always room for grace. Let's not let our heavenly Father get mixed up as a burden rather than a blessing. He is our greatest hope, our most faithful Companion, and our sweetest love.

In those quiet moments between the heartbreak and holy, Mozie Bear reminds me of my loving Father. He meets me in the darkest moments, and He lays there with me, just like my little bear. Let's be careful about mixing up the blessings and burdens and remember the true and precious gift those things are. The good always outweighs the inconveniences. The things we often mix up as burdens instead of blessings are often the things that point us to our Creator and show us peace in unexpected places. They're the little messengers that remind us that it's OK.

ENTRUSTED WITH THE OUTSKIRTS

I think it's easy to look at where we are and think of where we wish we were. It's easy to think we're not where we want to be. I can think of so many seasons of my life when I wished it had looked different. I grew up as a dancer. I went to dance most nights of the week, and I spent long Saturdays at competitions and rehearsals.

There were tons of talented dancers at my studio. Every dancer was grouped with their level for dances. The highest-level group in my age division always had dances together. You were naturally closest with the people you were in dances with since you spent so much time together. I was in a bit of an awkward spot between the groups. I was in some dances with one group of dancers and some with another. I was split between the two levels. I was the only one who spent half my time with both groups. In both groups, I was the odd one out. I didn't fit in like the rest. I didn't know all the inside jokes, and I wasn't invited to the birthday parties or sleepovers. I was always the one caught in between and left without a space. I always felt like the one on the outskirts, watching from the outside. At the time, it caused me to really dislike going to dance. I just felt like no one noticed I was there or wanted me there. It came to the point where I would wear only dark clothing instead of all the cute dance clothing I had collected over birthdays and Christmases. I no longer wanted to be noticed. I always claimed my spot in the back corner of the class. I just wanted to blend in. Then I wouldn't have to try to fit in.

Looking back at that season, I see the blessing it was to be entrusted with the outskirts. It was a blessing to be the one without a place because I could meet the others on the outskirts. It was the biggest blessing because I learned the outskirts had its own company. The most uncomfortable place to be was the exact place I was needed. Maybe that's the case for your season too. Maybe we're not where we want to be, but that's where we're needed. Being in between the groups allowed me to reach out and be in both groups of dancers. It expanded my friend group. I may not have been very close with either group, but I got to love more people.

I definitely didn't have an "outreach mindset" from age seven through high school. At that point, I was more bummed by where I was. I just wanted to fit in. My closest friends became those who were also on the outskirts. There only a few of us, but we needed each other. A few of them had also adopted the mindset of blending in. We always met in the back corner of the room and in across-the-floor lines in the back of the room. We would meet each other in the same places, day after day, and we eventually began to develop a comfort together.

We helped each other find peace in unexpected places and on the outskirts. Seeing the in-between spaces as a burden was one of my biggest mix-ups of that season, and not belonging was one of the greatest blessings. I was able to belong with more people—even if it was just as a mere presence and not necessarily as well-developed friendships. That may not have been where I thought I wanted to be, but that's where I was needed. If I had fit in one of those groups, I wouldn't have noticed or seen those on the outskirts. The outskirts were such an opportunity and a meeting place for those who were wandering. On the outskirts, we had each other. On the outskirts, everyone belonged and had a place.

God never mixes up the blessings and the burdens. He knows He has us where we are needed; it's all a blessing of transformative holy work loaded with eternal purpose. In some seasons, we're entrusted to meet those who have no place. Maybe He's entrusted you with a similar role in the season you're in. Caught in the in between is where you'll meet those who are looking for their place too. Together, you'll find peace in unexpected places. Together, you'll find, even here, on the outskirts, it's OK.

LOTS TO LEARN ABOUT LOVE

I have a lot to learn about love. I often have a lot of gaps that need filling in terms of how I can love people better. Thankfully, I have many people in my life who continually teach me so much about love through the grace and generosity they offer in their friendship. I have a whole lot left to learn—a lifetime and a half worth. One person in particular has taught me a thing or two about love, and he rarely uses words. His name is Steve.

Steve was my judge during the Miss Illinois competition. He

was the reason that interview was the toughest of my life. He was the head judge of the pageant, and I give him a bunch of credit for my success in winning that title. Throughout the interview, he was diligent in peeling back the layers to see me as I was—the girl under all the glam. Since the Miss Illinois pageant in 2018, I've seen him once. However, almost every month for years, he sent me a handwritten letter. I regretfully admit that I've probably only responded to two of the letters. He's even sent me multiple high-price-tag, thoughtful gifts out of the blue and without reason. He is the most kind, thoughtful, and genuine person. Despite my lack of response and correspondence, he continues to give so steadily. He is a clear picture of grace and has so many characteristics of Christ. Even though I continue to fall short in my side of this friendship, he continues to show up.

The time, effort, intentionality, and cost of his unwavering steadiness in our friendship doesn't scare him away—not to mention the time and distance we've spent apart from one another. It would be easy to see the letters and gifts as too much time, too much effort, or too expensive, and it would be understandable. He could easily see it as too much of a burden, but he sees it all as a blessing. He doesn't get it mixed up. He sees the value as worth the cost. He doesn't see the burdens; he sees the person on the other side, and all his intentionality is a way of investing in and blessing another person. Steve is a part of my life in all the ways he can be. I'm so honored to be on the other side of his kindness.

I think we all have a lot to learn about loving people. Let's find all the friends we look up to in our lives and work on loving people a bit more like they love us. Love is meant to be shared. I think Jesus is and always will be the One to look to for what a good friend looks like. He was especially good at being a friend to difficult people. He loved the people He knew would let Him down, and He continually showed up for people. He wept with those who wept, and He rejoiced with those who rejoiced. No matter how much people let Him down, He showed up. He saw the value as worth the cost—in every single person. Even with all He navigated with people, He didn't mix up the blessings and burdens. He didn't see those investments in relationships as burdens; He saw them as blessings. He saw the person on the other side.

As easy as it would be, Steve doesn't mix up the burdens and the blessings. Friends like Steve reflect Jesus in the ways He continually shows up full of grace. Let's be more like those friends.

Chapter 6

VANTAGE POINT

TUCKED AWAY A LITTLE FARTHER DOWN THE INLET FROM THE
Malibu Club in British Columbia, Canada, is a place called Beyond
Malibu Base Camp. Similar to the Malibu Club, the only way to get
there is by seaplane or boat. Beyond Malibu leads high schoolers on
weeklong backpacking trips to summit the surrounding mountains.
Base Camp is where all the equipment and meals are stored and
prepared for each week of campers. Base Camp only has one building
with electricity, which is powered by a nearby waterfall. The rest of
camp is life as it would be without technology. The bathrooms
are outhouses, and there is one outlet for the entire staff to share.
Beyond Malibu strips away all the distractions that often fight for
our attention, and it takes people back to the simple life.

Every week, the Base Camp staff and guides welcome a new
wave of campers and leaders. As the campers file in, boat by boat,
all the campers are rallied together, and the guides do a fun little skit
to explain what the week ahead will look like. They also announce
the mountain each group of campers will be climbing. Campers are
broken into the groups they came in, and guides begin to distribute
equipment for the trip. That night, all the campers, leaders, and their
guides spend the night at base camp in their lean-tos (basic shelter
structures) and begin bonding with their guides. They pack their
packs properly and ensure they have all their meals and equipment,

which ranges from ice axes to gasoline for the camping stoves. The next morning, they head out. They board a little boat, make their way to the base of their mountain, and begin the trek.

I've had the opportunity to do Beyond Malibu twice. The first time, I had no idea what to expect. I figured it had to be a bit of a glamorized version of camping, which is exactly my type of camping, but I was in for a treat. I'm that girl who brought a rolling suitcase to Base Camp. There were no paved pathways or elevators—just rocky trails that lead to the lean-tos. Base camp was along the lines of what I expected, but the trail experience was not.

We showed up to the start of our route, and it was just a rocky beach before the thick forest began. There were no clear paths, trails, signs, benches, or outhouses. There was just a mountain above us and a path that I couldn't see. We began to hike, and every other step, I was whacked by brush and cobwebs.

Within hours, our bodies were as beaten up as our expectations. We were hiking through thick brush in the summer's heat, single file, each following the steps of the person in front of us. We were all quietly processing our expectations of the experience versus the reality of what it was turning out to be. We were about eight hours in, and the energy of our guides made it obvious we were nearing our first campsite. Just outside the perimeter of our campsite, we were in "beehive territory." The area we were walking through had beehives in some of the trees. To walk through that territory, we separated about ten feet from the person in front of us, and we walked through as quietly as possible in an effort not to disrupt a bee colony. It was difficult to follow in the footsteps of the person in front, being so separated, and it was nerve-racking at times because it was tricky to be sure you were going in the right direction. I was intentional about staying calm, listening to the person in front of me, and trying to watch for rustles in the bushes.

As we were making our way through bee territory, one by one, we had to climb over a huge log to continue on the path. It was important not to take too long to avoid losing the person in front of you. Naturally, I took the beached whale approach over the log. I quickly realized it was a bad idea as a novice hiker with a sixty-pound pack that towered over the top of my head. I was too far in to go back. As I was lying there, stomach and body flat on the log, I began to circle my legs around to the other side to hop down.

As I was placing my feet on the ground, proud of my success in that questionable approach, my feet didn't stop at the ground. Before I knew it, I was dangling in a huge hole. My backpack was caught on something and kept me suspended. I was too afraid to look down or see how far the drop would be. I decided to sit there in ignorance until the person in back of me arrived. She did, and we shared a silent chuckle in my terror, and then we began to figure out what to do. She was assessing where I was caught. My pack was stuck on a part of the log, and the only way to get unstuck was by using my momentum to jump down into the hole. I was expecting a five-foot drop, but it was thankfully only about a foot. I was standing in a den of sorts. I didn't want to look around too long in case there were eyes looking at me as their bedtime snack. Once I had my feet on the sloshy, muddy ground, my pack was unhooked. I was able to put my elbows on the sides of the hole and hoist myself up to the forest floor.

What a way to start my first backpacking trip. All my expectations were thrown out the window in every single way. A few steps later, we made it to the first night's campsite. Funny enough, in order to get to the "BIFF," the bathroom in forest floors, we had to crawl over the log again. I went once and held it the rest of the time. Beyond Malibu Backpacking now knows the giant hole on the other side of the horizontal log as "Grace's Hole." I guess I was the first and last to ever fall there. What an honor!

When I took my tumble in Grace's Hole, I was stuck by something I couldn't see. It took another set of eyes to see what was keeping me there. I think that can be the same in life. We get stuck by something we can't see, and it takes a different vantage point to help reveal what it is and how to get unstuck. With God, we have another resource to help us see all the things that might keep us stuck. We can use the Bible as a mirror for our lives. When we read and come to know and believe the truths of God, we begin to recognize the things that don't align with His Word. Those things that don't align may be clues into what may be keeping us stuck. Maybe we need a different vantage point to see the things that we didn't see or didn't realize were keeping us held in place. Taking on that different vantage point, whether it be the Bible or a friend, gives us the perspectives needed to help us see where we're stuck. They see what we can't and allow us to cover more ground in depth and space.

Whether in bee territory or dangling in a den by what you can't see, a different vantage point will help you find peace in the most unexpected places.

PERSPECTIVE

A marathon is a long, long way. I'm speaking from experience. Three miles is a long way too, also speaking from experience. I began training for a marathon seven months prior to the race. I started with about a mile run. I stopped and walked halfway through, and I was going at a very slow pace. A mile just felt like a long way. As my training progressed, so did my ability to run. At the start of my training, I wasn't able to make it through a mile at what would later be my recovery run pace.

My mileage built by the week. Every week was a little more. Regardless of the distance, my mindset was steady throughout. I penny and dimed my way to the end. My currency for penny and diming varied, but my mindset remained. Sometimes I'd tell myself, "Just turn the corner," "Just get to the shadow," or "Just get to the bench." It was always something in sight that felt easily attainable and something I could reach quickly. Once I got to that point, I picked something new to reach. It was like rock climbing with my mind. Every step is progress, and forward progress is all it takes to reach the finish.

Running taught me a lot, but during my marathon training, words escaped me most of the time. It was like I was fully present in each run, but more often than not, I was just present in the run and nowhere else. I was just penny and diming myself through each route, which actually brought me to be completely present in my reality.

The morning of my long training runs, I would always write on my wrist: "Don't resist." I did not want to resist my present reality; instead, I wanted to lean in and embrace every piece of it. Resisting takes too much energy and causes us to miss all we have to gather from each passing breath. I didn't want to miss a moment. As I would look down at the smudged ink on my wrist, I would take in my five senses. I would bring myself to that exact moment. I would read my body, see where there was pain, intentionally release tension or worry from that area, and allow the pain to lift. On some long runs, I'd go without headphones and listen to all the sounds around me. I even did that during my marathon. The present moment is a sweet place to be when we're willing to just be where our feet are.

If I had begun the marathon thinking, *Wow, I have twenty-six miles left,* I'm not sure I would have made it. I just started by eyeing down mile 2. And with a one-mile run, I eyed down that first quarter of a mile. I couldn't think of it all at once. Bit by bit, piece by piece, running taught me to put my palms up when I'm in pain. Adopting a posture of praise and perseverance in the midst of pain takes practice. That was a great space to practice. Every run I took, it was one breath, one step, one hill, or one mile at a time. That's what got me through.

As I was further along in my training, the days of six miles and under felt like nothing. Those were my "chill" rest runs. Now, three miles is a long run for me—and plenty challenging. It's all about perspective. When I was six months deep, training to run 26.2 miles, anything short of ten miles was a treat. If you would have asked me how I felt about a three-mile run near my marathon, I would have been thrilled and questioned if that even counts as a run. Now, three miles is about my max. It's a long, long way. Our vantage point determines our perspective. Regardless of distance, my mindset stayed the same. I penny and dimed my way through the whole thing. Every mile is different throughout a run. The first mile can't determine the next. The terrain and feel are dynamic; even how we feel during each run continually ebbs and flows.

Whether it was one mile or 26.2, from the vantage point at that current moment, both were a long way. At the time, I was ready for them. In this season of my life, three miles is plenty, and that's mentally manageable for me. Our vantage points vary from season to season and so do our perspectives. There is no need to get caught up in how different one is from the next. Seasons aren't meant to look the same. Once we recognize that our vantage points will change every season, we'll find peace in unexpected places. Bit by bit, breath by breath, step by step, and mile by mile, we allow ourselves the freedom to find that—regardless of what this mile or season looks like—there's peace to be found.

STIRRING UP DARKNESS

To become a certified scuba diver, a deep dive was required. Our group had gathered at the surface, and we were getting ready to descend forty feet to the deepest part of that particular Illinois lake. We did our buddy checks and began to release the air from our vests.

As we descended, we had to stop every couple of feet to equalize (release pressure from the nose, ears, and mouth since the water pressure increases with depth). The water was getting darker and colder. We were continually checking our depth gauges. Once we hit forty feet, we would begin to ascend. All of a sudden, the water began to cloud. I couldn't see the person next to me. Our fins had stirred up the lake floor. It was pitch-black. There was no light. I was disoriented, and I couldn't tell which way was up. I reached out and tried to touch my buddy, and then I felt her grab my arm. We did not know which direction the surface was. Our instructors had stayed above us, where we were supposed to stop, and they were above us enough to have more light and enough visibility to see what was going on. They descended to where we were and began to inflate our vests enough to take us in the right direction toward the surface. Once we began to ascend, the darkness began to fade. We could see again.

The vantage point the instructors had over us offered peace in unexpected places. When we couldn't see anything at all—or even tell which way was up—they understood the situation. We had gone too deep and stirred up the bottom, and we couldn't figure out which way was the surface. Their vantage point gave them a clear view of what happened, and they knew exactly what to do to help us.

Think about God's vantage point. It must be amusing to Him how often we go too deep unintentionally. We get lost. We get disoriented. We stir up darkness, and then we no longer know which way to go. He sees everything from above. He sees what happened, how we got there, and how to solve it. When we're lost and reaching out, hoping to find anyone, He sees us exactly where we are. He comes and meets us there.

God's vantage point sees the big picture. He knows what we need and when we need it. He meets us in those places, and He shows us which way to go. No matter how deep we've gone, no matter the mess we've stirred up, and no matter how dark it is, our heavenly Father sees us. He offers peace in unexpected places, and His saving light and grace continually remind us that it's OK.

Chapter 7

ACCESS POINT TO AUTHENTICITY

THE AMOUNT OF TIME I'VE INVESTED IN PICKING A PICTURE TO POST is embarrassing. Let me take you through the steps. I take about ten times too many pictures, and then I go through and heart all my favorites. I have the hardest time remembering to go back and delete all the other pictures I didn't use. After that, I take my favorite picture, pull up about three different editing apps, and edit the picture in each to see which one I like best. Finally, I go back to Instagram and click on my favorite edited picture and then click through all the other edits and filters to see if any add the light, lines, or feel that I'm looking for. Then, I put my phone down and brainstorm likable, commentable, and creative captions. The driving force behind all of it is telling the story I want other people to read and know about me. However, really, outside of that posed picture, edit, and filter, there's likely an entirely different story to tell.

I create a post that tells people what I want them to know and what I want them to believe. I let them see what I want them to see. Whether that picture happens to catch just the right moment where I have a thigh gap, my arms look thin, or whatever else it could be. Whether I'm happy, thriving, figuring it out, or calm and collected, I create the content to reflect the story I want to tell—regardless if that story is my reality. We use all sorts of methods to hide the bad and amplify the good. The motives that I put into practice way too often are the reason why social media spaces can be unhealthy. They become a platform for filtered and amplified versions of our realities—with a twist. They are hidden, amplified, and filtered enough to tell just the story we want everyone to know.

Here's the kicker, and I'm talking to myself here too. Real talk and an unfiltered look into our lives develops peace in unexpected places. They offer other consumers a breath of fresh air and someone to relate with in a space that's easy to see as a space of competition and comparison. When we offer vulnerability by authenticity, we're inviting others to do the same. When we allow others to see the true reality of our lives rather than telling people the story we want them to know, we allow people to see the mess and the miracles. Vulnerability is the most powerful tool we have to offer.

Social media is a space where people gather, regardless of where they are in life. It's a gathering place. They can gather silently or loudly. They can gather as a contributor or solely as a consumer. So many people gather in that space for their own reasons. We've all mindlessly scrolled. In that space, there are people experiencing their highest highs and lowest lows, and their posts might look very similar to each other. Those at their highest highs may share it openly, and those at their lowest lows may tell a story they want you to see. What an expressway to produce discontentment. What if we had the courage to just be real and let down our guard to authenticity even in that space?

One of my favorite quotes is by Morgan Harper Nichols: "Tell the story of the mountain you climbed—it could become a page in someone else's survival guide."

We really don't know who is at their rock bottom, mindlessly scrolling and searching for any resemblance of hope to hold onto. Let's try to share our realities with that person in mind, the one at rock bottom, to inspire that person to keep going. We can remind them that they are needed and seen. May the content we offer and the realities we share enable those dwelling on rock bottom to see their lives as worth living.

Our authenticity tells the story of the mountains we've climbed, and it may be a light and sweet hope to those on the steep parts. People need to hear your story. You've been entrusted with your story to share it. Welcoming others into your true reality lets them in on all God is doing and has done in your life, including the mess and the miracles. My dad always says, "Don't deprive the world of who you are," which includes letting your guard down. Be an access point to authenticity. Create a space where others can find peace in unexpected places and believe that—no matter where they are—it's OK.

A Part to Play

For a brief bit of life, I was part of my university's marching band as part of the dance team. I had no idea what I was doing when I joined the team. I came from a strictly dance background. A good portion of the dance team was marching. We marched in football pregame shows and halftime shows. Every week, a ton of hours went into the halftime show. Every halftime had us marching in formations and making different words and shapes, which required us to learn a new set of steps and drill charts. Each individual in the band, close to four hundred people, had their own unique path and set of steps for every formation. Every person needed to do their part in order for the formation to come to fruition. Again, this aspect was very foreign to me. I had never seen a drill chart before band camp ahead of football season. The drill chart told us our coordinates at different periods of the halftime show.

The entire band would practice for hours and hours every week to ensure each person would get their coordinates memorized and executed perfectly in addition to the mini routines we had at certain points while marching. It was a lot to process. I navigated my coordinates and marched according to my drill chart's directions, but the directions and steps seemed completely random. It would be six steps to the right, a sharp turn to the left, four more steps, and so on. Marching your own steps, which were often different from everyone else's, seemed almost pointless. I thought there was no way these random steps were creating anything. I'm sorry to admit that I usually dreaded practice because I didn't believe I had a part to play. I didn't think my role mattered.

From an aerial view, it was always the coolest formation. A formation we hit every week in pregame was the outline of the United States. I was always along Oregon's coastline. I knew my exact steps and placement to reach that point every time. I knew my role, and I knew I had a part to play in the big picture. Every individual did.

When we're telling the story we want to tell, it's usually with a pretty narrow perspective. We only see our immediate moments and maybe a small circumference of the surrounding time frame. We don't see the big picture; we just see our immediate reality. What if we tried to consider the big picture? God knows your past, present, and future and the integral part you play in a bigger story.

We do all we can to create the lives we want. We learn from the past and use it to shape the future. We have a white-knuckled grip on our lives and what we want our realities to be. Some of the most difficult things to process are our expectations that go unmet, processing and healing from what we thought life would look like versus what it is. As I told myself during marathon training, don't resist reality. We're continually becoming and processing through who we are. Don't sweep the tough stuff or the unwished-for realities under the rug. Acknowledge them face-to-face. Process through them, let yourself heal, and welcome them into part of your story. Even in the moments when you still don't understand, you have a purpose and a part to play in the big picture. The Bible is like our own drill chart. It leads us in the direction of our purpose and calling. Even the pinky toes carry great value in the body of Christ. You can trust that no little step in your life is without intention.

It's like those mall directories where it says "you are here" with a little star. While you're walking through the mall, it's hard to tell where you are, but when you look at the map, you see the big picture and know exactly where you need to go to get where you're trying to go. God and His Word are our references for those directories, and He will show us where we need to go to accomplish all He wants to accomplish.

God is good at using the moments we feel had no purpose or gain for our good and His glory. The more access you give God over your life, the more power He'll seep through your past, present, and future. It begins with letting go of the story you want to tell for the story He has for you. The life you're living right now carries eternal magnitude. He wants to use the tiny pieces, the monumental moments, and all the in-between times, mess-ups, heartbreaks, and hurts in miraculous, holy, and impactful ways. They are essential parts of your story.

Once we let Him have control over those things, He'll begin to reveal the bigger picture. The steps you've taken are not pointless. They're packed with purpose. Let them be an access point to authenticity. Hold onto the hope of the little steps. The little steps you're taking now are part of a bigger story that our heavenly Father has written with the utmost care and intention. This hope will help you find peace in unexpected places. Our loving Father's plans for your life are bigger and better than your wildest dreams.

THE BIG PICTURE

My mom taught my brothers and me how to knit, beginning at a very young age. We usually just knitted scarves. They were pretty straightforward. We were creating something one stitch at a time. Every stitch counted. Throughout the process, I frequently messed up and lost a stitch or two or three, which would leave a little hole in the scarf. As a young, novice knitter, there were holes everywhere. Once I finished the scarf, it was long and thick, and I was sure it would do its role well. When I looked a little closer, I'd see all the holes and mistakes. If that's what I looked for, I found a whole bunch of them. From a distance, instead of seeing all the holes, I could just see the full scarf and its purpose.

I think it's easy for us to do the same with our lives. Let's say our lives are the scarves we're knitting. We look in really close and see all the holes and mistakes, and we forget the bigger picture and point. What if we took a couple steps back and saw the bigger picture? What if we let the big picture make space for grace? What if we saw the growth instead of the gaps along the way? There's always a bigger picture that puts everything in perspective. Let's keep life in perspective. Keep what you're looking for in check. Through all the gaps and growth, there is peace to be found if we look for it.

SCARS HAVE A STORY TO TELL

Scars have a story to tell. Maybe they remind us of a reality we could have done without in our lives. I have a couple scars, and they all have a story. The little crater on my forehead is from chicken pox; my triplet brothers and I all had it at the same time for forty days (bless my parents). The scar on my elbow is from accidentally setting my arm down in broken glass. I was in middle school, and it was late at night. I didn't want to wake up my parents, and I super-glued the cut closed. It didn't heal as well as it probably could have. I have another mark on my arm that's from bumping into a pan of salmon right out of the oven. I have scars on my fingertips from a couple bad burns.

My family and I were playing our own rendition of a cooking show. I accidentally set my fresh-out-of-the-oven pan with parchment paper on a burner with a flame, and it caught on fire. In order to prevent the quick spread of the fire and my lack of foresight, I grabbed the hot pan to pull it away from the flame. I quickly realized that was a bad idea. A few seconds later, I was met with pretty intense pain, and a bit later, some plump blisters developed. Weeks later, they were a cross between scars and calluses.

All of my minor and silly scars have a story to tell. They're like little memory badges. Some scars have a heavy or scary or sad story to tell. They might be the kind of story you don't want to be reminded of, whether or not they've even left their mark on the surface. Those with scars that have left a mark far deeper than the skin might see them as reminders of those moments of deep hurt. If no one has told you, I'm sorry. I'm sorry for the scars those moments left that still reach soul level. Would you believe me if I told you your scars could save? Jesus's scars do, and He'll use yours too.

Those scars may have inspired and influenced the direction of your life. Look how far you've come. If you don't like the direction you've come, you're not stuck. A season is not your story. When you see those scars, tell their story. There is no need to hide. Let them be an access point of authenticity and an access point to the other side of the story. Let those scars remind you of the hope you found in the hurt and the hurt you made it through. We can redefine what those scars stand for. They can stand for survival, strength, and tenacity. Let the scars take you on a journey of healing and forgiveness. Bit by bit, we can wash away the pain that they once harbored. Let them be symbols of hope for all that's yet to come. If you "tell the story of the mountain you've climbed, it could become a page in someone else's survival guide" (MHN). Your story and your scars are sacred. Regardless of how shallow or soul deep they are, there is hope. Your scars can save someone who is going through something similar. There's purpose in your pain and refinement in the fire.

The scars on Jesus's hands and feet offer new life that can heal any scar on the soul or the skin. We have a source of hope, and we can be a source of hope. Let's take on our bravest posture of vulnerability and offer our true stories—not the ones we want to tell, but the ones our scars tell for themselves. Your vulnerability could be the first access point to hope and healing to someone with their knees on rock bottom.

Offering your story, your scars, and your courage paves the way to finding peace in unexpected places. Even in those places of hurt, before the healing—when the scars are fresh and still taking their place on your soul and skin—there is hope. There will be another side to the scars someday. They will tell a greater story of hope, healing, and redemption. Let the scars tell their stories. Let them be access points to authenticity.

Chapter 8
WHAT ARE YOU LOOKING FOR?

AT ONE POINT IN MY LIFE, I WAS CONVINCED THIS GUY I WAS talking to was the perfect guy. He was kind, handsome, and genuine, and he loved the Lord. We talked for a good while and went on dates. I often thought, *How do you get better than this?*

For some reason, I lacked interest. He was so polite, chivalrous, and traditional. He was honorable and treated me with the utmost respect. He seemed like the perfect guy. *How can I not like him? It must be a me thing.* I struggled with walking away from him when I was convinced there was something wrong with me for not liking him. Since I believed I was in the wrong, I stuck around and strung him along for a disrespectful amount of time. I was in the wrong there. I was told he was everything I could ever want and that he would take care of me. It all sounded so good, but I still couldn't get on board. I finally walked away. In all honesty, it took a couple times before it was for good. I don't believe in "perfect" matches or "perfect" people. I believe in finding your person.

Then someone shared some wise words: "I had to let him leave my doorstep so he could go to someone else's—and someone else could come to mine." My doorstep had to be empty for someone else to approach it. It took letting him go before anyone else could stand in his place. I had to let him leave my doorstep. And when he did, my doorstep was empty—for a long while. It caused me to question

52

if I should have ever let him go and if anyone would ever come. I questioned a lot. I had to practice trust in the waiting. There was peace and purpose to be found there. The seasons between someone on your doorstep are still packed with purpose. Just because it may have been longer than I wanted or looked different than I thought, that season holds its own sacredness in my story.

The fact that the "perfect guy" and I weren't a match has no influence on or correlation to who I am or my worth. He could have been perfect in every way to someone else. He deserved to have someone who believed that. He deserved more than I could give. It came down to what I was looking for. On paper, he was everything, but when we interacted, I quickly knew he wasn't a match. For a long time, we tried to fake it. *How could it not work between us?* I would fall asleep at night, knowing he wasn't it.

It kind of makes me think of picking a vacation spot. We could paint the picture of two vacations and label each itinerary as the "perfect vacation," but two people could choose differently. They are still both the "perfect vacation." It depends on what you're looking for. I would choose a mountain over a beach and a lake over the ocean. That might not be your cup of tea, and that's fine. We're both still left with our "perfect vacations." In order to choose one, the other "perfect vacation" had to be turned down. Perfect is different for each person, and it is completely based on what you're looking for. We have to be careful with what we're looking for. We have to be careful not to look for our savior in people. Those expectations will crush anyone you place them on and leave you disappointed. Only Jesus can save.

I didn't like the perfect guy because he wasn't *my* person. We weren't a match. I had to let him leave my doorstep so that he could go to another person's doorstep—and so another person could come to mine. I had to welcome the unknown and learn to find peace in unexpected places. There, with an empty doorstep and a table set for one for a long time, I found peace and purpose. I learned I was OK there—just as things were.

Life really is what you look for—even with your person. If they're not your match, let them go to another person's doorstep that really wants them there. Maybe you'll find a new face ringing your doorbell someday, and maybe it'll be your person.

Searching for Community

Churches weren't meant to have walls, but they're often a space we all gather in each Sunday. Moving off on my own was a long-term search for a church and community. At some points in my life, I went with my family and sat with my family. When I moved to a different state, I went alone and sat alone. It allowed me to really see what seemed like a good fit for a church. Before evaluating anything, it was important to consider what I was looking for and ensure that what I was looking for was what God would deem of value. I began to consider what was influencing what I look for in churches—and in all things.

I was raised in a slightly smaller church setting, and because of that, that's what I gravitate to. Most importantly, I want a Gospel-based church that loves God and loves people. The churches I tried but didn't go back to did not feel like home to me. There was usually nothing wrong with them, but they weren't what I was looking for.

I tried a whole bunch of small groups in an effort to get connected in the church and community. I've been part of a couple small groups, college groups, and a hybrid group of sorts. They were wonderful. I also really enjoyed an all-girls group. The search continued for me, and I held tightly to my friends and family throughout the process.

Just because something isn't what you're looking for, doesn't mean there's anything wrong with it or you. It comes down to what you're looking for—as long as you continue to consider what those influences are. Among all you're looking for, look for Him first and most. During the search, there's peace to be found in unexpected places. Our Father sees you, and He'll meet you wherever He's invited. And whether that is sitting alone at church or sitting with a community, you'll find that He's there and always has been.

THESE ARE THE GOOD OLD DAYS

One of God's sweetest blessings and greatest displays of grace in my life has always been my family. Being a triplet is being born with built-in best friends. My parents cultivated this desire and delight in just being with each other. I learned how much I love the word "with" from my family. All I ever want to be is with my people. It breaks my heart to think that this isn't everyone's reality. For some people, family is a heavy word that brings up a place that's still healing.

I don't take for granted the blessing that my family is and always has been. My parents love to remind people that there's always a seat for them at the table. On many Sunday evenings growing up, most tables in our home were filled with people eating a yummy, home-cooked meal. It offered such a clear image of what I believe our heavenly Father's table looks like: filled to the brim, yet everyone has a place. I believe our heavenly Father's table is long and overflowing with people and joy, and there's room for everyone. The sweetest truth is that there's a seat for you. There's a place setting with your name at His table. You're always welcome there—just as you are.

That's what my family's dinner table felt like. With all the busy schedules of a household of four kids, my parents tried to have dinner together at least once a week. That space was a holy place. Our phones didn't tempt us as distractions because of the joy, delight, and excitement we had in being with each other. Some of my favorite memories of all time come from that space. How sweet it was to wake up in a home, warm with the love of a family that cared about how you slept and the day ahead. How sweet it was to count down the minutes of school or work to get home. How sweet it was to come home to a family that greeted each other with hugs, snacks, and questions of the day. How sweet it was to sit around a table for a home-cooked meal with people who delighted in being next to each other and had been looking forward to that moment all day. How sweet it was to fall asleep in a home that was safe and sound and filled with the people you couldn't wait to see the next morning. How sweet it was. Thank you, Jesus. To this day, we remain close, although life looks a bit different. We now get to look back on those days as the good old days.

Life evolved, as it always does, and our family life has been a bit reimagined. Even years and years since those days, I still grieve over what life is when thinking about what life was. That sounds sad, but I think it's part of adjusting to the new and settling into life as it continually evolves. These days, I look a little harder for the good. Everything is a bit heavier, yet it is still holy. I've slowly been adjusting and recognizing this version of life is sweet too. We can't spend so much time thinking about what life was that we miss the goodness of what it is. These are the good old days too. If we look for the good here, we'll find it.

How sweet it was to move away from home without knowing anyone and getting to build a life in a new community. How sweet it is to wake up next to Sweet Mozie in a space I've made my own and with a heavenly Father who is always with me. How sweet it is to go throughout the day, knowing I'm capable of handling whatever is thrown my way and having a God who will help me in ways I didn't even know I needed. How sweet it is to invest in a yummy meal, nutritious food, and a pretty table setting with a candle—even when it's just set for one. How sweet it is to fall asleep, cuddled up next to Mozie, and have faith that we can sleep in heavenly peace because of our Father's protection. How sweet every season is when we look for the good. Thank you, Jesus.

These are the good old days. Don't miss them. It's OK to grieve over past seasons and all the ways you're still processing through what you thought life would be versus what it is. No matter what life looks like, right here, right where your feet are, there is good if you look for it. When we do, we'll find peace in unexpected places—just as things are. Let's choose to live each day believing this version of life is worth living and knowing that these really are the good old days. Here is packed with purpose, peace, and good if you look for it.

LOVING PEOPLE

One of the greatest honors of winning Miss Illinois was the people I got to know and work with throughout the year. One individual I got to work with, we'll call her Jane, was one of the most difficult people I've had the opportunity to love. She knew her craft well. In fact, she was the best of the best. I knew what a privilege it was to work with her, and I also knew she could be a tough critic at times. I was very intimidated by her, and she was very blunt. It was part of the pageant gig, but we're all human. Some of it was still hard to hear.

Jane and I ended up getting to do a lot together. We spent a ton of time together: traveling, sharing hotel rooms, and prep sessions at her house. We were around each other a lot. With time, I began to get to know her, little by little. I learned about her past, her family, and her hopes and dreams versus her reality. She had a complex relationship with her family, and her parents struggled with health complications. The complications caused them to leave out a filter, and perhaps some harsh dialogue took place. She had been deeply hurt by those who were supposed to love her most. So much hurt was harbored in one heart. Hurting people hurt people, even unintentionally. Learning her story—and beginning to understand why she was the way she was—disarmed any tension, anxiety, and intimidation I had toward her.

As I got to know Jane, she became a true joy to be around. All my intimidation and anxiety around her was disarmed by understanding why she was the way she was. She'd been hurt, over and over. She was working through life and trying to hold herself together, and it happened to rub off on her advice. I wonder how many Janes we come across in life. How often are we the Jane to the people in our own lives, hurting people unintentionally because of our past hurts.

Let's lean into loving difficult people. They're the ones who need it most—even if they don't know it. Let's show up for them with an open ear, intentional questions, and a presence that is consistent. Get to know them. Get to know their stories, little by little, and you'll begin to understand why they are the way they are. You'll begin to see traces of the hurts that have poured over them. Let their stories disarm any negative sentiments you've carried of them and make room for grace.

We can choose to look at them for what they've done or who they are and the stories that have shaped them. When we choose to see them for who they are and the hurts they're healing from, we begin to find peace in unexpected places—even in loving those we find most difficult to love. Soon enough, they will become a true joy and a delight to love. We have a source of love in Jesus, and we can be a source of love too. Love can go a long way toward healing hurting people. Let's find the difficult ones to love, lean in, and see the good in them.

Chapter 9

TEND TO YOUR GARDEN

I'M A HORRIBLE PLANT MOM. MY PLANTS MUST HAVE IT THE WORST. I probably wouldn't have a lot of plants, but my mom loves them and continually graciously gifts them to me. I used to not water them at all, and some still survived. Eventually, enough deceased plants down the road, I finally decided I would do my due diligence to take care of the plants. Once a week, I try to give my plants a bath. I know that's still probably not nearly enough care, but I'm getting there. As a result, my plants are looking a bit more lively. I hadn't done a great job of taking care of my plants because I saw caring for them as a burden. I tried to shift my mindset. I thought, *These plants have been entrusted to my care, and I'm going to be a good steward of them and tend to them.* It really does take pretty minimal work to care for a plant.

I dove deeper into my thought process. My plants are a natural analogy to the things we're entrusted with in this season of our lives. Every season looks different and has different priorities and things to care for. No matter what this season looks like, let's be good stewards of what we've been entrusted with. Tending to something is dynamic. It looks different with each day. Tending to the field you're in begins with recognizing the things in your care—what you've been entrusted with—and then showing up, assessing the needs, and caring for those things.

Part of caring for plants is pruning them. By taking the dead leaves off, the roots won't send energy and nutrients to something that no longer needs it. Pruning keeps the plant healthy and makes room for new growth. It almost reminds me of haircuts. I highly dislike haircuts, but I know they are the key to keeping hair healthy. They promote growth. Let's do the same with our lives and make room for new growth.

Rather than seeing the things we've been entrusted with as a hassle, let's see them as part of the field we've been given to tend in this season. We must consistently prune them to make room for growth and cut off the old to make room for the new. If we're faithful in tending to the fields we're in, with time and care, we'll see the growth that happens just from showing up.

Chapter 10

THE PURPOSE OF A SAILBOAT

LIFE IS HOW YOU LOOK AT IT. IT'S AMAZING HOW MUCH WE CAN shape our realities based on our interpretations of all that's thrown our way. It comes down to how we learn to handle life. Whether reactive or proactive, whether we stare down the problem or stare down the solution, life happens to you—or you happen to life. The sweet thing is that we're built for this. We're built to handle the hard things. We're built to be able to see a problem and develop a solution. We're built for the tough stuff.

At one point in college, I decided to take a college course in sailing. I wanted to learn how to sail. To be honest, the main reason was so I could get the unique position as a sailing instructor at the Malibu Club. I took the class, and most of it was actually sailing. We would go out on an Illinois lake and take the sailboats for a spin with an instructor. I wasn't great at sailing. I'm sure it was entertaining to my instructor, and I definitely kept him on his toes. Most of the time, I was very nervous. I knew I had a lot to learn, and a lot of close calls were ahead of me.

When the winds picked up, my heart rate did too. High winds are the call to action in sailing. You have to know where you're going to know how to respond. You must read the winds from the jib and tack accordingly, depending on where you're trying to go. I'll let you in on a little secret here: I usually didn't pay a ton of attention to where the instructor told me to go. My only goal was staying afloat—no matter where the winds took us. If I had known how to operate the sailboat properly, I would have been able to take us where we were supposed to go with the help of the winds.

A sailboat is built for the winds. That's where its true purpose shows itself—if the operator knows how to use it properly. I was so consumed by all the wind and waves that I forgot the entire purpose of a sailboat. I was merely riding the winds and waves. If I had operated the sailboat as it was intended to be used, the winds would have made us thrive. I was holding it back from its purpose.

How often do we do that with other things in life? If we had enough faith in God and ourselves to do what we've been built to do, we'd save ourselves a lot of time, worry, and energy. What if we happened to life?

Let's not get so caught up in our reactions to things that we forget to be proactive in handling them. We don't need to spend so much energy on how we feel about the things that happen to us. Instead, let's focus on how we're going to handle them. The cards will always be dealt, but you decide how you play them. Just as a sailboat is built for the winds, you're built for the tough stuff too. There is no need to focus on the winds when you're in a vessel that's been built for them. There is no need to focus on the problems when you've got a mind, a body and a Father that were built to handle them. The winds will come, and you decide how you will weather them.

God has authority over the wind and waves, and we can rest—no matter the height of the swells or their strength. Life is how we look at it; let's look at all we were built to do. When we do, we'll find peace in unexpected places.

TATTERS TELL ALL

Within the Miss America Organization, you have to win a local qualifying pageant in order to go to state. My first pageant competing in the oldest age division was a pageant I hadn't planned on competing in. The board for that pageant reached out and asked if I would because they were short on girls.

At the time, the Miss America Organization scoring criteria was 35 percent talent, 25 percent interview, 15 percent evening gown, 15 percent swimsuit, and 10 percent onstage question. It ended up being a pretty solid group of contestants. Many of them had competed at Miss Illinois and even placed in the top five. I knew it would be a tight competition. It was a one-day event, and there were about eleven girls. Throughout the day, we had rehearsals, and that night was the pageant.

Since it had been a very last-minute decision to compete, I was not very prepared, which goes against my grain in just about every way. The day before the pageant, I had gone to a dress store and picked out my evening gown, interview dress, and heels to go with both. I had done mock interviews with my family in the week leading up to the pageant. A few nights before the pageant, I had a solo choreographed to use for talent. I had about two days of training with it before I was performing it on a stage. I borrowed a costume from a friend, and I had my brother take a picture of me against a wall for my headshot. I was up against veteran competitors who had their wardrobes from the previous year's state competition. The girls all seemed to know each other and were quite talkative. No one talked to me, and I didn't really talk to anyone either. I was intimidated.

In the morning, each of us competed in a ten-minute press conference-style interview, and just about anything could be asked. I was confident I could hold my own. About three girls at a time were taken outside of the interview room to be on deck. My new shoes were not very comfy. I brought flip-flops to walk around in, and I carried my heels in a bag. I was just planning to put them on right before heading into the interview.

As I waited, the anticipation grew. I saw every polished and professional contestant walking out of that room with such confidence and ease. I was finally on deck. I stood outside the interview room, took a couple deep breaths, and did a few final touch-ups in the mirror. I took my new heels out of the bag to switch out my flip-flops. The beauty of the heels made up for their discomfort. They were so pretty, neutral, strappy, and minimal. As I was putting them on, my foot slipped right through. I looked closer, and all the straps had been cut through. There were clean cuts through every strap on the heel.

I looked at the other shoe and saw the same thing. There were clean cuts through all the straps. I was about a minute away from having to walk in for the interview. I decided I'd just go barefoot. There really were no other options at that point. Luckily, we got to stand behind a podium.

A young woman was introducing the contestants to the judges one at a time, and she noticed my bare feet before opening the door. She quickly and quietly asked what happened. I told her, and without hesitation, she took off her heels and said, "Here, wear these." Bless her heart! I walked into the interview with shoes on my feet.

The rest of that day didn't exactly go as I had hoped. I got first runner-up, which is second place in the pageant world. I learned a lot that day. I learned that life is how you look at it. I could have seen the lack of interaction as unwelcoming, but I chose to see it as intimidation. If someone is intimidated, they know your ability and power and see you as competition. In the end, it is really a compliment. I chose to see the cut heels, however that happened, as a demonstration that I can handle whatever is thrown my way. I'm built to handle the tough stuff. I had the opportunity to let life happen to me and sulk in response—or I could happen to life, stare down the solution, and be proactive.

God is our enabler. He can empower every moment to be a

time of refinement. When we choose to see every moment as an opportunity for growth, every moment is a gift. When we adopt that mindset, whether there are clear cuts through the straps of our shoes or things just aren't what you thought they'd be, we can find peace in unexpected places because life is how we look at it.

IF THE ARMOR FITS

Over the years, I've grown to love a story in the Bible. By no means am I a theologian or even someone who knows the Bible as well as I should. This story was explained to me so clearly that I've just hung onto it, and I have learned from it throughout multiple seasons. It's the story of David and Goliath. Every day, the Philistine Goliath stepped into the battlefield and was ready to take on anyone who would face him. If someone defeated Goliath, the Philistines would be under the Israelites' power. If no one took him down, the Israelites would be under the Philistines' power. None of the Israelite soldiers would step forward to go head-to-head with Goliath.

One day, a young shepherd named David stepped forward. David had no experience in battle, but he was a young man of great faith. Goliath, on the other hand, was huge and had been a warrior since he was a kid. He was rough and aggressive and out to kill. Before stepping out to meet Goliath, David tried on some armor and put on a helmet. He walked around with it for a bit and decided he wasn't comfortable with it. It didn't fit right, so instead, he took what he always had with him as a shepherd: a slingshot and some smooth stones.

As Goliath began to run toward David to attack, David ran toward him, grabbed one of his smooth stones, and slung it right at him. It sunk into Goliath's forehead, and he fell to the ground. David had done it against all odds—with nothing but faith in God. He believed if God would deliver him from lions and bears as a shepherd, he would deliver him from Goliath too.

I love that David stepped into battle with nothing but what he already had. My pastor said, "If the armor had fit, it would have gotten the glory." How true is that? David and every witness to this miracle would have given the credit for the victory to his protective armor. Since he just went out with what he had, God got the glory.

It's easy to forget to praise God when we think we did it ourselves. David didn't get that mixed up in this instance. He didn't need special training, special weapons, or armor. It was just what he already had: his slingshot and faith in God. David saw God instead of the enemy.

Life is how we look at it. Let's learn from David. Let's step into each and every day with our eyes on God instead of the enemy. We've already got all we need for victory. When we believe it and live like it, we'll find peace in unexpected places—just like David.

PART 2
RECOGNIZING PEACE AND ITS OPPOSERS

Chapter 11

MISS ILLINOIS FALLS SHORT

SO MANY THINGS IN LIFE WILL DO ALL THEY CAN TO RUFFLE OUR feathers and disrupt our peace, but nothing can if we don't let it. We will still experience the highs and lows of life, but through all of it, we can have peace. I think about coming home from Miss America. Going to Miss America is a dream that so many little girls have their whole lives, but only a few will walk away with that national sash across their shoulder. So many people walk away from that dream to find a new one. In the moment, it's a harsh reality.

Miss America was a sixteen-day experience in Atlantic City, New Jersey. It was held at Miss America's original location, Boardwalk City Hall, where it began in 1921. In those sixteen days, we had TV production, rehearsals, media days, appearances, and all phases of competition. My roommate was Miss Wyoming. Bless her heart—she was a soul unlike any I've met. She had an aura of kindness, joy, and peace. The best part of the experience was the people I got to know. One of them is still one of my very closest friends: the most brilliant, genuine, wise, compassionate individual who we referred to as Miss South Dakota.

In our final week there, the competition began. First, we all competed in a ten-minute, press conference-style interview, one at a time. It was an opportunity to make an unforgettable impact on the judges and be selected into the top fifteen. I approached that week with the primary goal to impact the other contestants and the judges. I knew I was on eternal assignment, and maybe I would be their first access point to Jesus.

Throughout the experience, I felt such a peace. I knew I was there to impact and not impress. I could bring a strength instead of a striving. When I thought something didn't go how I'd hoped, I kept thinking, *If the armor would have fit, it would have gotten the glory.* God would do what only He could regardless of my performance. Following interview, I competed in onstage question, evening gown, and talent. Talent was my sweet spot. I was a lyrical dancer, and performing was my safe space where I could let my guard down. It was the place where I felt like I had the most to say, yet I didn't have to use any words.

Once we got to finals on Sunday night, I was nervous yet at peace. I knew I had performed well, but I also knew that only God's plan would become reality—no matter the dreams, hopes, and prayers that culminated in that night. God's plan is what we would pray for if we knew the big picture.

I had the sweetest community backing me throughout my time leading up to Miss America, and the most generous crew was in the audience throughout the week and for finals. I felt the strength, power, and peace of all the people who had led me to that stage. Every time I walked on stage, I imagined every single one of them walking beside me. They were my army. With Jesus, they were the sum of all I was. What a force! I got so many pictures and messages from all the watch parties taking place on finals night. It was the most supportive and generous community.

On finals night, I stood on the Miss America stage and held the hands of the women next to me. All of us were waiting to hear if we'd get one step closer to this lifelong dream by making the top fifteen. I took a deep breath and looked at the American flag on the back wall of the hall, which was about a football field away. I just thanked Jesus. I prayed, "If You're willing, I pray for a spot."

One by one, they announced the spots of the top fifteen.

Fourteen contestants were one step closer to their dream. As I stood there anticipating the last name to be called, I prayed, "Jesus, You say whatever I ask for in Your name, I'll receive. So, Lord, I pray for a spot in the top fifteen, in Your name, Jesus. Please Jesus." I stood on the brink of my dream, unable to do anything more. It could end there—and it did. The next name was not mine. I thought, *It must be a top sixteen.*

As the hosts dismissed all the non-finalists, and everyone around me began to leave the stage, I followed. I caught a glimpse of the eyes around me, filled with tears, and I realized mine were too. I sat down backstage at my makeup station where just a few minutes before I was the closest I'd ever been to my biggest dream. Now, I was on the other side of it. For a while, I just sat there. Not much went through my head. It was just all too much. I let myself just rest there in the moments between the thoughts, trying to process the reality of what had just happened. I didn't want to. I couldn't. *What else is there to think about?* It was all I had been thinking about and dreaming of for so long. I didn't know where to direct my mind to, but it couldn't be there. I just let myself sit in stillness.

A couple hours of competition went by, and a new, incredible Miss America was chosen. It was time to see all the people who had come to support me. In all honesty, I felt such embarrassment. I was so embarrassed that so many people had followed the journey, flown out to be there, and gathered to watch at home—and I had fallen short. I was sinking deep in disappointment. I had forgotten the gift of just being there. Yet, in the exact state I was in, I was covered in such love.

The next day, I got on a plane to fly home. I was happy to just be with my people, in our place. For a little while, we could just process and rest. I happened to come across Monday morning's headline, "Miss Illinois Falls Short," which was followed by a front-page article about my shortcoming on the Miss America stage—for all the community to read. It was a twist of the knife. Even so, there was still peace. I knew the capacity, depth, and focus of the experience. It was an eternal assignment that the world wouldn't be able to grasp, but I knew my heavenly Father would do what only He could.

It took me months and months to process that reality, bits and pieces at a time. Little by little, that dream settled into its place in the past. The excitement of dreaming a new dream grew. There are so many things that try to disrupt our peace. Nothing will—if we don't let it. Let's shift our focus to impacting people instead of impressing them. Let's bring a strength rather than a striving. This shift lets us rest in a holy assurance that we're on eternal assignment to be an access point to Jesus. Even on the brink of our longest dreams, we'll find peace in the thick of disappointment, and see our Father in everything rather than ourselves.

TRAINING FOR 26.2

Training for a marathon definitely came with its ups and downs. It was a large time investment, and running is hard. It always has been, and it always will be. It is a unique space though. It is an appointment with yourself. It is time set aside to focus on our instinctive habits of breathing, being, and making it through.

So many strategies evolve as I trained. I followed a beginning training plan. It was about sixteen weeks long. At first, the runs were between three and five miles. The goals for three miles were to get the first mile done, then a mile and a half, then two miles, then two and a half, and so on. The goal changed as I went on. What felt and seemed long changed as the training progressed. At first, five miles was a hefty run—and a big accomplishment for me. Then, once I was running six to nine mile runs on weeknights, a six-mile run felt like a piece of cake. It was all about context and perspective. Running was hard at three miles, and it was hard at twenty. My strategies remained pretty consistent: "Just turn the corner," "Just reach that shadow," "Just reach the bench," "Just reach the light," and "Just get to mile two."

Running taught me to be present and focus on one breath at a time. The climate of the run would change. *How I feel in this mile doesn't reflect how I'll feel in half a mile or in fifteen miles.* Regardless of the distance I had ahead of me, I still took it one step, one breath, and one mile at a time. Whatever was in front of me in that mile and moment became a milestone. Little bit by little bit, I celebrated the milestones amid the miles. It kept me in the present moment and added meaning to the miles between my feet and the finish line.

I learned that I could find peace in the midst of the pain and discomfort. There was a "more" to tap into. Part of tapping into that "more" came with not resisting reality. I had to fully welcome the reality of the moment, the discomfort, and the weight of each step. Each step would carry me further. I recognized all my five senses, and I rested there. I carved a place for peace in the pain and rested in the fullness of my reality.

In the heavy and hard moments and miles, when the milestones came slowly, I flipped my hands. I put my palms up in the pain. I wanted to develop a posture of praise in the pain. I think praise is just thanking God and recognizing His goodness in everything. I wanted to train myself that in my worst moments, my natural reaction would be to put my palms up. I think we have to practice the posture before the praise comes. So, in my lowest lows, I hope to be found with my palms up. If I'm practicing the posture, the praises will follow.

In life, we're always going to have opposing forces. In running and in life, we can always practice our posture before we find the praise. Then, we'll slowly find praises everywhere. Praises can be as simple as the sound of our steps, realizing that each step is progress, or noticing the sky or the trees. Whatever you look for can become praise. Praises can be the ability to breathe through anything or the ability to find praise in pain. We can start with the basic gifts we tend to forget.

Praise paves the way for perseverance. Gratitude disarms our resistance to reality and lets us see the good just as things are. It disarms all that's opposing our peace and welcomes it all as part of what can be seen as good. We can endure even the toughest times when we practice gratitude in moments that may not make sense: "God, thank you for this endless hill. Thank you for showing me that I can breathe through this."

There seems to be good everywhere through gratitude. In all the opposing forces we face, it all begins with our posture—no matter our pain. No matter what's ahead, look for the milestones before you. Whatever is in front of you, moment by moment, there is a milestone to reach. Every step is progress, and every milestone adds meaning.

Keep your palms up in the pain. Practice the posture even before you find the praise, and it will pave the way for peace and power. Look for the good with a lens of gratitude, and you'll find it everywhere. When we do, we'll find peace in unexpected places— even while running a marathon.

THE GUY WITH THE SIGN

My brother and I spent our second semester of our sophomore year of college in New Zealand. Saying goodbye to our family and our other triplet brother when leaving home was the most difficult part. We would be gone for seven months. We had a long journey ahead of us—and a nineteen-hour time change. We flew from our local airport to Chicago, Chicago to Dallas, Dallas to Sydney, and then Sydney to Auckland, New Zealand.

Our leg from Chicago to Dallas was very delayed. We knew this would cause problems for our next leg, the big leg from Dallas to Sydney. We had even built in plenty of buffer time. We boarded the plane long after we were supposed to. During our flight, we were watching the time. We were going to be arriving after the last call for our next flight. Someone sitting next to us overheard us strategizing how to make the next leg. They began to chime in—and so did the person across the aisle and the person behind us. A flight attendant rounded out our kind and selfless strategizing team. We were landing in an entirely different terminal from where our next flight was leaving. It would require a train and a bus. If we missed the flight from Dallas to Sydney, the next one was three days later. Complicating things more, we had mixed and matched our airlines. We had to make the flight.

When we finally landed in Dallas, everyone in front of us let us get off ahead of them. Our first step in the airport was a sprint. To our surprise, the first person we saw was an older man with glasses, a vest, and a whiteboard: "Benjamin & Grace." He said, "I'm here to help you get to your flight. They won't wait for you. I'm just here to help. You better run."

So, with our loaded fifty-five-liter packs on our backs, we ran. He would yell instructions for where to go from behind as he followed us. As we arrived at the gate, they were closing the doors. We squeezed through the door, and we thanked the guy with the sign as much as we could. We had made it. Everyone else was already settled, and Benjamin and I found our seats and took a breath. We quickly sent our last texts to family for the next seventeen hours.

We took an interesting approach on our adventure, and we arrived a month before the semester began to explore the country. We stuffed our backpacks to the brim. I was quite proud of myself as an "overpacker." I wanted to prove to myself that I could survive with only the necessities, and that's what we did.

We finally arrived, and the experience of a lifetime began. With the backpacks on our backs and no plan to follow, we began our journey from the top of New Zealand to the bottom. We started in Auckland on the north island, and our destination was Dunedin, which is near the bottom of the south island. By foot, bus, boat, train, and friends made along the way, a month later, we made it to our destination—one campsite and hostel at a time.

Sometimes I think God uses people to create peace in unexpected places. Our seven months in New Zealand began with a strategy crew on our flight from Chicago to Dallas and a kind, unexpected guide waiting for our arrival, each and all helping us get to our destination. In the context of faith, let's not overlook the people in our lives who have helped us get one step closer to our destination. Our home is heaven, and our citizenship is in the King's kingdom. Let's notice those people who are helping us get there. The strategizing crews and the unexpected guides may help with one step, like catching a flight, but that gets us one step closer to home. We get a glimpse of Jesus along the way. Let's notice those people and praise Jesus for placing them there. They point us in the direction we're supposed to go. Let's be more like those people.

Chapter 12

UPROOTED

THERE'S SOMETHING SWEET ABOUT THE UNFAMILIAR. IT CAUSES YOU to cling to the familiar. While my brother Benjamin and I were in New Zealand, I experienced this to its full capacity. I held so closely to everything I was familiar with. However, I have a weird tendency to love leaving my comfort zone and doing things I never thought I would do. I think I like to prove to myself that I can. You know how when someone tells you that you can't do something, it encourages you to respond, "Watch me!" I do that to myself all the time. And before I think too much about it, I'm doing it. I've had this interesting quirk since I was very little.

When I was three years old, I rode a horse for the first time. It was one of those little farms where you sit on the horse while someone walks it very slowly in a pasture. I got to do that on a beautiful foal. I remember how proud I felt. I loved horses. Not too far into the pasture, a passing motorcycle spooked the horse. It bucked its front legs and ran, and I rolled off its back. The next thing I remember was lying in my mom's car. I woke up to her face right over mine.

A few weeks later, I was enrolled in horseback riding lessons, and a few years later, I was in a horse show. From that experience, I wanted to learn how to ride. I wanted to prove to myself that I could get back on a horse, unafraid, and know what I was doing. From what I can remember, that was the first time this interesting quirk was put into action.

Let's take this story back to New Zealand. As a complete homebody and family gal, I would have been the last person on the planet to ever imagine leaving my home and family for any amount of extended time, but I was about as far away as I could get from home for seven months. Talk about uncomfortable. I held closely to every bit of home I had with me.

My brother Benjamin is a fearless adventurer, and for the most part, I'm quite the opposite. He was a tough one to hold too closely because he was thriving. I usually couldn't keep up with him. I found myself holding closely to my backpack, passport, phone, and a necklace that my other brother Christian got me before I left. It had the coordinates of home with a Bible verse. When I say I held things closely, I took it a bit far. I slept with my phone and backpack next to me and my passport and necklace around my neck. I just wanted home—and all I needed to get home—with me at all times. I held onto all the traces of my roots that I could carry with me.

We got to experience so many sweet memories during those seven months. We had plenty of moments with no place to stay and no way to get somewhere. One experience reveals just how uprooted we were. Peter was a volunteer at a famous little chapel in Tekapo. He watched as guests shuffled through the little church, and he would open and close the property.

Benjamin and I took a bus to Lake Tekapo, and we were staying at a campsite a few miles from the church. There really aren't taxis in Lake Tekapo, and we were not savvy about any ride apps. I doubt they were present there at the time. Benjamin and I mainly got around by walking. We made our way to the church and shuffled our way in. We sat down in the pews and enjoyed the beauty of the space, looking through the front glass at the beautiful mountains and lake. It was a sweet time to recognize the same God we held closely to at home was the same God with us across the world.

When we were making our way toward the door, we met Peter.

He stood by the door in a dark button-up shirt and jeans. His gray hair fell over his face a bit. We started talking, and he told us his role there. He asked us where we were from, why we were there, and where we were headed.

After talking a bit more, I guess our uprooted state was rather obvious. He graciously offered us a ride back to our campsite. We happily accepted the offer and jumped in his little black car with all our stuff. He had to run a couple errands along the way, which honestly made me nervous. In the end, we arrived back at our campsite.

We ended up seeing Peter the few times we visited Lake Tekapo again. It's sweet how generosity always leaves its mark and makes the farthest places from home seem a little bit familiar. In the midst of the unfamiliar, the power of a friend was on display. Familiarity began to grow for us in that little corner of the world. The church, our campsite, and Peter all became familiar bits to hold onto along the journey. We made friends at the campground too, and they offered us a ride on their jet skis. They were airline pilots from New Zealand.

We also made plenty of bus friends. We were all on a journey to and from somewhere, and our paths intersected for a brief moment along the way. What a gift those in-between moments were and the commonality that we were all uprooted. We were all finding the familiar in the unfamiliar, and soon enough, that became each other. We were all headed to different places at different paces, yet these temporary encounters always carried such value and a long, impactful shelf life. One woman we met on the bus was from Texas A&M. She and I ended up emailing frequently for about a year after our brief intersection. She was a devoted follower of Jesus—out to love another uprooted heart she met on the bus—and I'm honored to say it was me.

So many things in life make it seem like there's a wedge between you and your roots. I think the enemy is amused by seeing how uprooted, isolated, and alone he can make us feel. God delights in putting the enemy in his place by using His people to make the most unfamiliar places seem a little more familiar with the people He places there.

Being uprooted allows us all to remember and cling to the traces of our roots we're able to carry. For some people, it may be a backpack and a passport, and for others, it may be memories. There's common ground in unfamiliarity. We're all holding onto something that offers the comfort of familiarity. Regardless of what it is, we're all a little more willing to love and lean into the unfamiliar when we find we're not the only ones there. God uses people to make the unfamiliar feel familiar. When we notice those people and offer a willingness to lean in, even in the unfamiliar, we begin to find peace in unexpected places.

EVICTION

The idea of uprooting may be attractive to the enemy because it makes us doubt our purpose in that place. It can be a quick and easy way to disrupt our peace and disqualify our presence. The feeling of being uprooted was a common feeling throughout New Zealand, yet it was met by many sweet gifts that made that country feel a bit more familiar. We don't have to be across the world to experience the feeling of being uprooted. I lived in Dayton, Ohio, in an apartment that felt like my home away from home. I loved it. It was a space I made my own. It was my safe space. It was filled with everything that made it feel cozy, and it was nestled in a sweet little neighborhood of lots of families. It was a beautiful area. I really loved it.

The only issue that seemed to show itself was the change of management at the apartment. In my two years there, there were three different management teams, which meant the logistics of living there changed frequently, including how we paid monthly costs, office hours, and the price of rent. It was a bit of an ongoing mess.

On three different occasions, because of the frequent changes in how things were done and the price of rent, I found a pink paper taped to my door. It was an eviction notice, which was not a fun thing to come home to. It almost always greeted me when I was coming back from a trip out of town. It was always a sweet surprise. I took the warning seriously every time. It always told me I had three days to leave unless I paid the new price. Every management team was seemingly great at making people feel uprooted. Every time a notice was left on my door, it was resolved rather quickly. In the following days, I found myself questioning my purpose in that place. I was always stuck on that pink paper, upset about the price increase, and wondering why their first way to inform me of the changes was a pink paper stapled to my door with a request to leave the premises.

It made me wonder how uprooted Jesus must have always felt. How often was Jesus unwanted in a place? The pink paper taped to His door came in much heavier ways—and eventually the cross. No matter the number of pink papers taped to His door, He didn't question His purpose in that place. He didn't fall for the enemy's lies to disrupt His peace, disqualify His presence, or dismantle His purpose. That pink paper told me I was no longer welcome or wanted in that place. It told me to take my stuff and leave or pay the price. Jesus set the example. He fulfilled His purpose wherever His feet were, and He eventually paid the ultimate price so we wouldn't have to.

The very people Jesus came to save are the same ones who told Him to leave. They are the ones who taped the pink paper to His door. Even so, He knew why He was in that place, and He didn't let that distract or disrupt. Let's learn from our Savior. Regardless of what that pink paper taped to your door looks like, whatever is trying to uproot you—whether people or closed doors—you don't need to be shaken. Don't fall for the distraction or disturbance. You're exactly where you're supposed to be right now. Hammer those stakes in where your feet are and live out the purpose you have in the place you're in. Jesus covers those pink papers in His blood. You're meant to be here. He died to know you, save you, and love you. He rose again so that pink little piece of paper would have no power over you. Uprooted or deeply rooted, you're equipped with eternal purpose in this place.

VICE VERSA

The feeling of being uprooted isn't always just from a place, but it can come from a person. During my sophomore year of high school, I had a big crush on a senior. We had been texting for a month, and I decided to ask him to his first and last Vice Versa (Sadie Hawkins/ Turnabout). I put a lot of thought into how I would do it. I obviously wanted to impress him. He was cute, and it was his first time going to a school dance.

National Pancake Day was approaching, and it was the perfect opportunity. For National Pancake Day, I was volunteering at a local restaurant to raise money for children's hospitals. I spent the majority of the day helping out, even missing school, and it was a great day. The butter and syrup on top of that day would be a date to Vice Versa. After a day working together, I had become buddies with some of the staff. I decided to include them on my plan to ask out my date. Prior to that day, I had kind of hinted at the idea of taking him as my date. He seemed hesitant but on board.

I had invited him to come get some free pancakes with my family that night. He came, and we all sat down together. Of course, we all ordered pancakes. As the orders came out, I had arranged for "Vice Versa?" to be frosted on his pancakes. Little did I know that my new staff friends would treat it like a birthday party. They all came out in a single-file line with his stack of pancakes leading the way. They had put a candle in it, surrounded the table, and placed the short stack in front of my crush. Everyone was taking pictures, and all eyes were on him.

He was not someone who enjoyed being the center of attention, but that's exactly what he was. He read the red and blue frosting on the pancakes and turned bright red. He was concerningly red. I would have done the same. He looked at me, looked down, tossed his hands up, and hesitantly said, "Sure!"

My mom pulled a plate of cupcakes out from under the table, and we all celebrated. At that moment, I began to dream of the night ahead of us. I'd wear my favorite dress, get to ride in his fast, red car, and walk into the dance with the cutest guy who had said yes to me. I was so proud and so excited.

When we left the restaurant, I was smiling from ear to ear. As I was beginning to settle in for the night, I was shopping for dresses on my phone. My phone vibrated, and I saw his name on the screen. I was so excited to see what he had to say about the night. I opened the message, and it was not at all what I expected. He could no longer go. I thought I'd be able to change his mind, but his next message said he was about to ask another girl to be his girlfriend—and he was no longer interested. Ouch. I felt embarrassed, inadequate, unwanted, and completely uprooted from where I thought I was with him. *Now what?*

It's easy to feel uprooted by disappointments—however they come—simply because you thought things would look different than they do, and that's OK. In those moments when we question why things happen, we can find peace in knowing that God is most careful with us. He works what we see as disappointments for our good. He allows the catalyst of the uprooting to be what settles us right where we need to be—and the very thing that protects us from what we hoped things would be—to make room for how things *should* be.

God always intercedes in order to work for our good and best, even at the cost of our hopes, because His ways are better. Just wait and see. He's most careful with us. When we believe that, even in our uprooting disappointments, we can find peace in unexpected places.

Chapter 13

THE NINE STARS

ONE THING I'VE ALWAYS FELT THROUGHOUT EVERY SEASON OF MY life is that I don't fit in. I don't think I'm alone in feeling that way, at least to some capacity. When I had friend groups, they typically seemed pretty short-lived. For a long time, I believed there must have been something off with me that didn't allow for the necessary bonds. I know that I'm not always very quick or easy to open up. I've always been that way. I know the closeness of my family played a huge factor as well. However, we're all human, we're changing every day, and people come and go.

There were seasons that this whole feeling of fitting in hit harder than others. One of them was growing up as a dancer. The dancers you spend the most time with are those you grow closest with. The top tier of dancers referred to themselves as the "nine stars," and they were. They were the most elite dancers in the studio. I was often placed in a few of their dances each year, which kind of made me an awkward tenth. There were a lot of days that I didn't know where I fit in. I was always intimidated to dance next to them because I knew how advanced they were, and I was afraid of being seen as the weak link. I needed to prove myself.

I would constantly contemplate the reasons why I didn't fit in. It all seemed to make sense when I came up with the reasoning in my head: "I'm not pretty enough. I'm not cool enough. I'm not as good as them. I don't have hair like them. I don't dress like them. I don't talk like them. I'm too quiet." My justification for dwelling on the outskirts was rooted in my own insecurities. I came up with all these reasons to validate why I didn't fit in.

Honestly, it makes me a little sad to revisit those thoughts and the lies I believed about myself. It breaks my heart even more to think of all the people who constantly have these thoughts. I think we've all been there. If only you could see and believe how special you are and how worthy you are. The difference between Grace then and Grace now is who I believed I was. I believed all those differences were the reason I was left on the outskirts. I now believe that those were the qualities I had been predestined with to set me apart.

We're all created differently because each and every one of us is created to impact people in ways only we can. Our differences qualify us. We need quiet people, we need quirky people, we need people who talk differently, we need differences. All the things you've pointed to as the reasons you don't fit in are the qualities you've been created with to impact the people God has placed around you. As you change, the people around you will change too—and so will your tools and the qualities that determine the degree of your impact. Next time it feels like you don't fit in, remember that you weren't meant to. The world needs you as you are. Let's embrace the qualities we once blamed and allow them to enable, empower, and expand our impact. When we do, we'll find peace in unexpected places—even in the moments on the outskirts.

OUTSKIRTS

A whole lot of my dance years felt like most of them were spent on the outskirts. I think a majority of my hours at dance were spent missing and wishing I was with my people. Every moment I was away from them, I felt like I was missing what mattered. I was always just trying to get back to my people. Bless my parents' hearts, but there were so many nights I'd call them from dance and ask them to pick me up. They had the discernment to tell me no. They knew I was where I needed to be. It was refining me. It was helping me grow and become. Even in the discomfort, they knew that was where I needed to be.

Just because I didn't feel like I fit in, didn't mean I wasn't supposed to be there. We will all have moments where we will be homesick and call our heavenly Father, wondering when we can go home to the place where we belong. He will lovingly keep us exactly where we are in order to accomplish what He has placed us there to accomplish. He sees what we don't see, and He sees who we don't see. As the One who holds authority over every heart, He works with such intention to equip and enable each of us to impact others.

Before the cross, Jesus asked His Father to consider if there was any other way. And even in His Son's discomfort, God—in His discernment—knew what needed to be accomplished. It could only be done where Jesus was, in the thick of it and on the outskirts. He wasn't created to fit in; He was set apart to impact. When He kept in step with His Father's plan, He could walk the path paved with perfect peace, knowing He was in the sweet spot of His purpose. We can do the same thing. In the moments we just want to leave, let's call on our heavenly Father. He'll help us live in the sweet spot of our purpose and find peace exactly where we are.

BACKED OUT

My dance studio days led me to some college dance days. For a long time, I dreamed of being a college dancer on the sidelines. During my senior year of high school, I traveled to several universities' dance clinics, and I even went to one audition. I loved that school, and I wanted to be a dancer there. I prepared well for that audition. If I made it, I'd be going there. I was cut in the first round. It was a huge bummer. After a lot of thought, I decided to go to one more audition at a different school, but I didn't prepare enough for the audition. In the final round, I forgot the entire choreographed dance that I performed in front of the judges with another dancer auditioning, but somehow—by God's grace—I made it.

The same feeling I had felt my whole life quickly arrived in this space too. I didn't fit in. I was confident God had something in mind. I knew He would do something only He could do. I struggled through that season. I felt unwanted, inadequate, and stuck. I felt exposed as the weak link and weighed down by social anxiety and fear. *How could this dream have gone so differently than I thought it would?*

During that first year, I left the team. It was a decision that felt so urgent in the moment, yet it took me years to find peace and healing in. *Had I quit an eternal assignment the Lord had entrusted me with?* To my complete surprise, a number of former teammates reached out and commended me for my decision and asked to meet over coffee. Maybe the unpopular move was one many of them had been gathering the courage to do. I believe in honoring our commitments, and that was a situation I worked through for a long time. When I felt helpless, God didn't slow down. He was still doing what only He could—even when I couldn't see it.

In our lowest lows, the Lord moves and shakes. He's doing what only He can. I would have gone about so much of that season differently, yet I praise God for how it all worked out. Where I lacked, He showed up. When I was faithless, He was faithful. It's a season I didn't understand until years later. I'm still finding the blessings the Lord gathered and used in that season. It was a much different season than I thought it would be, but God knew His power and purpose in it long before I ever understood His plan. In a season where I felt completely absent from the assignment He entrusted to me, He still did what only He could. His power isn't dependent upon our abilities. Lay down the rough seasons. Let Him show you what He's up to. Even on the outskirts, peace can be found in the most unexpected places.

Chapter 14

UNDOING

I was born with coarse corkscrew curls and thick, frizzy hair. I call it unmanageable, but those who have seen it call it pretty. As a little girl, it was adorable. You better believe I rocked the 'fro. I was proud of it. My mama told me it was beautiful, and I believed her. On vacations, my parents would have it cornrowed so it was more manageable.

Then, when I was around eight years old, I started hearing the comments. People would ask, "Why is your hair so poofy?" Little by little, I began to hide my hair in any way I could. At first, it was some up, some down, then it was a ponytail, and then it was a tight bun. I couldn't stand any "flyaways," and I began to use clips to hold every hair back. I would hear the kids in line counting the number of clips I wore in my hair.

I didn't know what to do with it. My hair didn't look like other girls' hair. No matter how I hid it, it was noticed in some way. Until I graduated high school, for the most part, it remained in a low bun. I remember going to hairstylists and trying to find someone who knew how to do my hair. Goodness, that was a journey. Many rough cuts and mishaps later, the far and few between rose to the top.

As I grew up, the hiding continued, but then I found the power of a straightener. It would take me hours and hours to straighten my hair, but it was a treat on occasion. Over time, I began to straighten it more and more, and I would get treatments to help straighten it more efficiently. Eventually the straight-hair look was my new look. It was smooth and professional. My later years of college, I always wore my hair straight to an internship.

One day, I mustered up all the courage I could find, and I went in with it curly. My secret hope was to get affirmations that this was how I should wear it all the time. Quite the opposite happened, and people suggested I go back to straightening it. From that day on, I never wore it curly to my workplace again. All the effort I was investing in straightening it was the basic expectation of how people thought my hair should look. As someone with fair skin, no one expected me to have ethnic hair. They said it didn't look right, and I agreed. I conformed to the opinions I heard loudest: wear it straight.

It wasn't an accident that I was created with thick, coarse corkscrew curls. It was written in my DNA. Nothing in creation is an accident. Each of us has our own qualities that make us different from the rest and offer their own set of differences and difficulties. For me, one of those differences was my hair, but it could have been something much different for you. How we're created is not an accident. We were created with intention and the most care. We spend so much of our lives undoing how God created us. In some ways, we may believe we're enhancing ourselves, but however you feel best is how you should give yourself the permission and approval to live. As we live, we may find ourselves recognizing the value of the unique qualities God created in our DNA, and maybe we can begin to embrace them rather than undoing them, little by little.

You no longer have to undo how you were created if you don't want to. You don't need to give others power over how you see yourself. Don't give them that power. Nothing about you is an accident. You were put together with the utmost intention. You were created as you are on purpose and for a purpose. Lean into it and live it out. Embracing your unique qualities might encourage another person to embrace their unique qualities. When I see a little girl with hair like mine, I always compliment and affirm them. They need to hear it. They need to know you can be beautiful and not look like the rest. In fact, there is beauty in that if we're willing to have the courage to embrace it. You are allowed—just as you are. You are seen, welcome, and enough—just as you've been created. When we begin to believe that, we'll find peace where we've never found it before.

FAKE LASHES

The Lord did what only He could when it came to my first job. As a journalism major, I was very unsure of what career path to take. As a requirement for my final journalism class, I had to create a reel and post it on YouTube. In the TV industry, that's pretty much a compilation of your best work and the first step to finding a job. Recruiters randomly look for reels and then email you if they like what they see.

Shockingly, I had my first email within hours of posting. My only intention in posting the reel was to pass the class—not get a job. After a couple interviews, and a little excitement, I became interested in getting a job. That was a new feeling for me. I even took my reel back to editing and began to add a little glam to it. I also did some research. I looked at the types of jobs within the TV industry, and I had my eyes on positions as an anchor or a lifestyle host. I was aware that I wouldn't be able to start as either of those, but I figured I had nothing to lose by trying. I sent my reel to every lifestyle show I could find. I honestly humored myself at the number of applications I sent and the market levels I took a shot at. I wanted to shoot my shot. I'm sure some of the people receiving them got some good chuckles out of it too.

For a couple months, I got emails and calls here and there. As I was getting ready to sign my first contract as a morning anchor at a small station in Texas, I got a short email from a different station that asked if I was still interested in their lifestyle host position. I jumped on it. They asked for a phone call, which was followed by a screen test on set two days later. A week later, I was offered the job. I had the day to decide. A few weeks later, I was moving to Dayton, Ohio. I was as nervous as I'd ever been. I was honored yet terrified to be entrusted with this position. *Do they realize I just graduated college? Do they realize I have minimal on-air experience?*

I thought, *Whether you're in the shallow end or the deep end, you're swimming. I might as well learn to swim in the deep end.* For my first two days of work, I came in heels with my hair and makeup done. I wanted them to feel confident in choosing me. On the first day, we began doing rehearsals on set with my cohost. They would tape the rehearsals and watch them in the control room.

After the first rehearsal, I was called into my manager's office with my executive producer. I was told I needed to do better. They knew I was a rookie, but I had to rise up. They acknowledged that my cohost had been doing this for ten years, and I needed to look like I had too. The next day, we rehearsed—and I felt like I had upped my game a bit, at least I hoped.

Again, I was called into my manager's office, and this time, a picture had been pulled up on the screen. It was a picture of me at Miss America. I had my long hair extensions, thick makeup, lashes, fake tan, the results of a yearlong diet, and a beautiful, tailored black dress.

My manager looked at me and asked, "Why do you look so different?"

I explained the degree of preparation that goes into looking like that on the Miss America stage. My manager said, "This is the Grace we hired. This is the Grace we expect to see every day."

From that day forward, I showed up to work looking as similar to that as I could—fake lashes and all.

I felt unwelcome as I was, but I was willing to rise up for the opportunity. When much is given, much is expected. I rose up. I was amazed that I got to work in a position that required heels, a dress, and fake eyelashes every day. At the same time, it challenged the way

I saw myself in the mirror. I became so used to seeing myself with fake eyelashes, full-faced makeup, and styled hair that I thought I looked rough in anything less. My standard for who I saw in the mirror had been conformed into who they wanted to see.

As time went on, I worked on remembering who I was before the job and before and after the makeup each day. I wanted that Grace to stay. It took practice to remember that who I was—as I was—was enough. I needed to remember there can be a both glamorous side and a more natural side. Both were equal in value and beauty.

No matter where I went, what I looked like, or how I was expected to look, I could find peace under the weight of expectations because I knew who I was.

Despite the expectations you're challenged with, your value is steady in the One who created you and your story. You're where you're supposed to be—as you're supposed to be. Let's practice remembering that.

Strawberry Blonde Hair

I've had my fair share of looks throughout my life. Some were on purpose, and some were not. They usually ranged by hair color, which was not on purpose. After four different appointments throughout my life, I have looked in the mirror completely concerned and confused.

The first time was a few weeks before my senior prom. I was told the highlights would help the straightening treatment take to the hair, but at the end of the process, I was a complete strawberry blonde. That was not a look for me. I knew it immediately. My stylist must have been able to tell my concern and immediately began to confirm that this was the plan and that I looked great. I was concerned. It was not, by any stretch of my imagination, what I had in mind, but that was that, and I walked out with strawberry blonde hair. It was a bit of a rough season aesthetically, including prom, and I eventually went to another stylist to bring it back to my natural honey-brown color. After turning around in that chair, my hair was nearly black. I was concerned again. Such drastic turns in color—and neither was the look for me. From there, I let the color grow and fade out.

A couple years later, after winning Miss Illinois, they wanted to enrich my natural hair color. Somehow, it was back to dark, dark brown. At the end, they confirmed that this was not their intention. They did all they could do to get the color out. It faded on its own. A slightly faded version of that dark brown was my color at Miss America. I actually really did learn to like it.

A few years later, I was told to get highlights for my look on TV. I went in, and I said I wanted them to be so subtle that no one would be able to tell I had them. I honestly just wanted to check the box that I had gotten highlights. By the end of that appointment, bright blonde streaks left a striped pattern across my head. I also had some fried-off remnants of bangs. This stylist was very unfamiliar with curly hair. At that point, nothing really surprised me. A few appointments later, someone was able to at least fix the color.

I've had a fair share of versions of myself, but time and growth have always brought me back to who I was at first. I could see the remnants of the changes that had happened, but the growth in my roots always reminded me of my true color. That growth was my hope through every mishap. I knew I'd be taken back to who I was with time. I had to let it all fade before I would see it again. I think we have to do this in life sometimes. Season by season, it's easy to get caught up in certain things. With time and growth, the commotion will fade—and then our roots will reveal who we are and who we were at first. Let's keep going back to that version of ourselves—the pure, untouched, original version—before we started trying to add all the dimensions and colors. Who we were at first was everything we needed to be and more. It was who we were created to be. Let the growth tell of how far you've come. The hope and peace you find along the way will expose the value of remembering your roots.

Chapter 15

BATTING CAGES

I WAS SOMEHOW CONVINCED TO GO INTO A BATTING CAGE AND TAKE a couple swings. I am very afraid of things coming at me, especially hard round things that could hurt me. I also have a hard time keeping track of those things. They move so fast, leaving me with a high likelihood of getting hit. I did it anyway because I like to practice bravery here and there.

I stepped in the batting cage, and the pitching machine was set to the slowest speed. It still seemed too fast to me. At first, I was about five feet from the plate. I didn't want to be anywhere near the strike zone. I was still trying to swing at it, hoping I'd somehow hit it. Behind the pitching machine, a professional baseball player was telling me what to do. I began to listen to his guidance. I was coaxed a baby step closer to the plate every time. And as I got closer, I began to make contact with the ball. I began to watch the ball. I learned where it was coming from and where it was headed. I learned its speed and course of action. As I got more comfortable with what was coming at me, I became less and less afraid.

Instead of clinging to the corner of the cage, I was up to bat. I was ready to play some offense. I think we need to do the same with the enemy. We often give him way too much power over us. Learn where his offenses are coming from and where they're headed. Learn his course of action. Get comfy with staring down his attacks, knowing you've got a Guide who sees and knows the enemy's schemes. That Guide is the One who conquered the enemy and holds all power and authority over him.

One of the most effective ways to protect ourselves is knowing the attacks are aimed at our weak spots. The enemy loves to act with strategy and plan his schemes around our most vulnerable moments. Don't worry—we're pulling the curtain back on him and exposing his ways because we don't have time to be the source of his entertainment. If it's a war he wants, oh boy, it's a war he's going to get.

We're in the midst of an intense game of battleship with the enemy, but it's a fixed fight. Jesus won it for us, but the deceiver will do all he can to convince you otherwise. He's got an X marked on your back. The enemy knows your power better than you do. That's why he's after you. He knows the power in you and the threat you are to his kingdom if you're not stopped or at least distracted and slowed down. Take it as a compliment, but in order to protect ourselves, we need to know our weak spots and the moments he will most likely try to come at us.

Jesus will guide you through every moment against the deceiver. He'll coax you up to the plate with boldness and obedience. When you learn the enemy's tactics, where he's aiming, when he attacks, and his course of action, he stands no chance. Step up to the plate, you know what's coming. Get ready to play some offense.

BODY IMAGE

One of the footholds I've given the enemy throughout my life has been body image. Unfortunately, for a whole lot of my life, it's been a very touchy topic for me. I know I'm not alone in this. Starting around seventh grade, I began to notice everything I didn't like about my body. I promised myself I'd never get "bigger" than the size I was. I wore young elementary clothes through most of middle school, and then puberty hit. I was resistant to any change from the beginning, which caused me to study and notice every inch of myself. As I changed, as anybody should at that point, I became more and more ashamed of my body. It looked different than it once did. I was holding onto a standard that was unhealthy and unrealistic.

As I grew up, the way I saw my body was a roller coaster. Most of the time, I was a slave to my image, ensuring my body was everything it was "supposed" to be. In my mind, it always fell short. I was too wide, too short, too thick, and too chubby. I'd get so frustrated. I talked so harshly to myself, always reminding myself of all I wasn't.

The enemy knew how to get in my head on this one. My body and food became a source of fear and shame. I did everything I could to hide it. Food became a dicey subject from middle school through college. I was embarrassed to eat around anyone. I was embarrassed by how much I ate. I tried to eat by myself when I could or wait until I was by myself. I was so afraid of certain foods making me gain weight. It became a heavy-shackled foothold and a long-term access point that the enemy had to my life. I'd try to listen to what the enemy was convincing me about and refute the attacks with truth. A whole lot of Jesus, restoration, and time did powerful work.

I'm still learning and figuring out my body. I've become increasingly better at celebrating my body and how far it's come and how far it will go. When I feel this war waging, I see the destruction of my past because of this foothold. I also feel the pressure of my Savior's hand on my shoulder. He is standing beside me. The war has been won. He packed this foothold with His power and healing. Jesus stands at the access point of this chink in my armor with His nail-pierced hands and feet, He is my protector.

One of my dear friends struggled with an eating disorder for years. She was a few years younger than me. One day, at a Young Life camp, we sat on a beach and had a real conversation over the brokenness in our lives, especially in this realm. We talked about the man at the healing pool in the Bible. This man struggled with infirmity for thirty-eight years. Jesus saw him lying by the pool, went up to the man, and asked if he wanted to be healed. The man told Jesus why he couldn't be healed, but Jesus told him to rise up and walk—and he did.

We often lie beside healing, restoration, and hope, yet we wait in our infirmity and think healing isn't an option for us. When Jesus offers to heal, we tell Him why we can't be healed. He whispers, "Rise up and walk."

Our Savior meets us where we are, and He offers to heal us where we never thought we could be healed. Saying yes to this healing and hope repairs the chinks in our armor. We have to be willing to believe that healing is available through our Savior and He will patch what was once a foothold with the truth of Jesus. He will use what was once a weak spot to become your thickest armor, patched by holy healing.

Look where the enemy is attacking you. Learn his tactics and schemes. Let's be so close to Jesus that we know how to read the enemy's strategies with ease. When we know where he's coming from and where he's headed, there's no need to be afraid. We'll find peace in unexpected places—even in the places that used to be the enemy's foothold. Let those become a part of your redemption story and ministry to others.

THE ACT

Another foothold the enemy figured out about me was my academic abilities, specifically when it came to standardized testing. Man, oh, man, I was convinced I wasn't smart. I'm aware that I wasn't the brightest crayon in the box, but I at least had a place in the box. For the longest time, I didn't believe I did.

Everything in school felt difficult. I battled this mentality from a very young age through college. It really became evident in my later years of high school. I always expected school to be difficult, and I always felt like I was behind in understanding something. Throughout high school, I would work on math or chemistry homework in a teacher's classroom for extra support. When I actually understood something, I thought I must have been doing something wrong. This lack of confidence caused me to have a lot of anxiety around tests. Anxiety caused me to forget just about everything, which proved to be problematic on the ACT. In fact, I took the ACT eight times. I took prep courses and had a tutor, but I had the same score every time. At least I'm consistent.

Part of the motivation for this was the college search process. I lived it up. I loved it and was so excited about it. I wanted to have as many options as possible. I applied to a lot of schools—way too many. The enemy had a solid foothold on this season because of the foothold he had on my beliefs about my academic abilities. Testing was where the enemy prowled at my doorstep. It was the height of my fear, anxiety, and low self-confidence academically. The enemy studied my life to know this area would be a chink in my armor and an access point for him. The way the enemy studies our lives to plan the most strategic schemes reminds me of the story of Jacob and Esau.

Jacob and Esau were twin brothers. Esau was born first. Esau was a hunter, and Jacob preferred to stay home. Jacob was cooking a delicious soup, and Esau came home starving. Esau begged Jacob for some of the soup, and Jacob told him he could have some if he sold him his birthright, which usually went to the firstborn son as a position of honor and double portion of inheritance. Esau said he was about to die and suggested a birthright was nothing to him at that point. He swore his birthright to Jacob for a bowl of soup, and Esau ate it up. A lot of strategy went into Jacob's scheme.

Jacob enticed Esau when he was most hungry. The aroma of Jacob's soup weakened Esau's wisdom and discernment. Jacob offered what he knew would sound best to Esau at that moment. Esau let a minute's temptation cost his life's inheritance and honor as the firstborn son. What sounded good for a night came at the expense of everything.

Don't let a minute's temptation cost you what you never intended to give. When we fall for the enemy's schemes, we give him access to that part of our lives, and he marks it down as a point of weakness to study. The enemy will entice us with what he knows we're hungry for at just the right moment. He's prowling at our doors. We must learn to stand firm in the truth we know and strategize with our Savior to be on guard.

Whether it is learning how the enemy strikes or learning our weak spots that he could see as access points, we have to always be on guard. The places where your confidence lacks may be clues into the chinks in your armor the enemy has found. He's studying and strategizing to find your weak spots because he knows the power in you. He can't risk letting you be a threat to his kingdom.

Our best shot at knowing the enemy's strategy is knowing our Savior's strategy. He's already conquered the deceiver and knows his ways. Lean into our King's truth and tactics. In Jesus, we are safe. We can stand, glancing back at how far we've come, with the Savior's hands on our shoulders, knowing it was because of Him. When we step up to the plate, ready to play some offense with the Savior of the world as our guide, we'll find peace in unexpected places. The deceiver can bring it on, but it's a fixed fight.

Chapter 16

NOT MY PLACE

IT'S IMPORTANT TO KNOW OURSELVES WELL SO WE'RE ABLE TO KNOW what we stand for. There will be moments that span seasons that will challenge our firm footing to sway or shift. The better we know ourselves, our purpose, and where we've come from and where we're headed, the better prepared we will be for the moments we're called to stand firm. That being said, I think we have a narrow view of the meaning of standing firm. I think it has a lot more to do with loving people and reflecting the character of Christ than we might think.

The older a student gets, the more often school brings moments where push comes to shove in what we stand for. Our nature and tendencies are collected in the minds of others, and our reputations, for better or worse, are formed. Our reputations, although probably very different according to who you ask, determine most offerings and invitations. I really don't know what my reputation was made up of. My involvement in things was across the board. In high school, I was very involved with sports and extracurriculars, but I ran solo most of the time. I was so across the board that I really didn't settle in with one friend group. I was a floater at best. In some ways, I think that served me well in many capacities. It was hard in moments, but it minimized the peer pressure I faced.

College was a bit of a different story. Again, for the most part, I was a floater with a few steady, precious friends. However, the peer pressure took things to another level. Joining a sorority, having a social life, and floating around friend groups called for their fair share of experiences. During my freshman year of college, I was out with a group of girls. The upperclassmen told about ten of us to line up. They said they'd pass a bottle of vodka down the line, and by the end, it needed to be empty.

However, I had never had an alcoholic drink before. My whole life, I've simply lacked interest in drinking. I didn't know any of the people I was with very well. I was at the end of the line, and I just tried to discreetly step to the side out of line. I was quickly seen by a few of the upperclassmen and questioned. They asked if there was some sort of religious deal for why I wouldn't participate—or if I thought I was better than everyone else. It was not a great spot to be in, and I left.

The biggest struggles I had when reflecting on that experience were the people I left there and the purpose I had in being there. Standing firm may include stepping out of line, but it also entails thinking about what your mission and purpose could be in uncomfortable places. For many, I think that experience was all just fun, and it was, but I remember it as the night I was challenged. My form of fun looked different than those in that situation, and since I was so focused on standing firm, I missed my purpose in that moment.

I kept my purpose to myself. I think I've done that a whole lot of my life, and it is a selfish form of defense. Standing firm is a willingness to exclude yourself from aspects of an experience, but it requires wading into the places where light is needed. We shouldn't keep our purpose to ourselves and leave; we should show others that there is another way. We should be a source of love and light in the places where those looking for both may gather.

I had a hard time finding my place, and that was a common trend that spanned seasons of my life. For a long time, I had a hard time understanding why it was such a theme. After years of processing through it and looking back on those seasons, my goal was never to fit in. A good amount of the time, I was resistant to settling in a lot of social settings because I felt on guard. I wanted to remember what I stood for, and I was afraid that what I stood for would be blurred if I was too comfortable or simply not welcomed. At times, I think that mentality caused me to miss my purpose in places.

Standing firm reinstates who you are in situations that are tempting you to shift. It also includes considering what your purpose is in uncomfortable places, especially when your light feels like the only one in the room. That doesn't mean you should dim your light; it might mean you're needed there more than it may feel. You're a light there.

Standing firm will look different for every individual. It all depends on the personal convictions in line with His truth and the gifts God has given you. In moments when you feel uncomfortable, lean in and love those around you. God is after their hearts. Standing firm is standing firm in the commission our Savior has entrusted us with—to love Him and love His people. Let's do that, everywhere, all the time. When we do, we'll find peace in even the darkest places.

TIME FOR A BREATHER

I was at my crush's house with some of his friends and family, and we were having a game night that turned into a living room dance party. That's my kind of dance party. At one point, I took my crush's hands and was pulling him off the couch. While I was really leaning back to counter his weight and pull him up, he let go of my hands. I took a good little tumble in front of his friends and family. I was embarrassed, and I tried to play it off and not take it too seriously.

A few minutes later, I needed to take my dog out. I left all the commotion and went outside. I began to process and replay what had happened, and I felt very embarrassed and a little upset. I started talking to God. I wanted to just forgive my crush and move on and be able to laugh at it once I got back inside, but I was embarrassed about being embarrassed. It was becoming clear that I really needed that little dog walk as a breather.

Talking to God about it made me wonder how often He has to take a breather from me. How often have I done something that wasn't exactly what He was hoping for or had in mind? How often have I not represented Him well and made Him have to take a breather? He's never left my side, but I'm sure Jesus has taken a large number of breathers from me. That thought fueled my grace. I thought about the amount of grace He's covered me in moment after moment. Grace upon grace. God uses moments like this to uproot things that we may not realize are there. Embarrassment is a reaction to disrupted pride. Maybe this experience was just one opportunity for the Lord to begin cleaning out that pride.

Standing firm includes remembering the character of Christ even when you don't want to or when it goes against your natural reactions. That's a good sign that the work of the Holy Spirit is shaping us to be more like Him one moment at a time—even when it requires taking a breather. Let it fuel grace. Pray it off, laugh it off, and know God is doing deeper work in you than you realize.

BREAKFAST WITH OUR FATHER

The greatest resource we have in all of life is God Himself. When we've welcomed Jesus as our Savior and King, the Spirit of God makes His home in us and helps us become more and more like Jesus. The guidance of the Holy Spirit leads us to live our most purposeful and fulfilling lives, and it gives us discernment and wisdom into what standing firm looks like in every season and situation.

Leaning into this relationship with God can seem intimidating. It looks different for everyone. As we spend time with someone, we get to know them more and more. Rather than hearing a lot about someone or spending time in similar circles, we know a lot *about* them. Truly knowing someone comes from spending time with them. It's the same with God, and the cool thing about Him is there's a whole book about Him. The Bible tells of His character, heart, and mission, which span all time. The Bible draws you in and helps you get to know God. I've always loved starting my day with Jesus. I wake up a few minutes earlier than I need to. In those moments with Him, I find promises and peace to take for the day. I always have enough of exactly what I end up needing. He prepares me for the day ahead that He's created and packed with purpose.

I've grown to think of those moments with God as breakfast with my Father. I imagine my Father downstairs, while I'm still sound asleep upstairs. He's up hours before I am. He's preparing all the favorites: cinnamon rolls, avocado toast, omelets, hash browns, fresh smoothies, and fancy imported coffee. He's setting the table with His best dishware and cutlery. He's preparing a place for us. He's counting down the hours and minutes until He hears the stairs creaking with footsteps. When He starts to hear rustling, He ensures everything is ready. He even packs a cooler to keep us full throughout the day. The table is full of all He's prepared, and He pulls out the chair, hoping we'll take a seat. He's got His eyes on the stairs. As we come down, He's got a smile from ear to ear. He's so excited to show us all He's prepared.

How often do we walk right past the pulled-out chair without acknowledging our Father who is so excited to see us and show us all He's prepared for us? Do we sit down, grab a few things, and go—forgetting to take the cooler?

How sweet are the moments when we take the time to sit down and hear and delight in all He's prepared for us. We are overflowing with peace, hope, joy, purpose, and the love of our Father giving us plenty to offer for the day. It changes the course of the day, and it changes us one day at a time. It transforms with love and delight in a new hope, purpose, and peace. Those moments with God look different in every season. For some people, it might be a devotional, reading a bit of His Word, journaling or praying, or keeping an open dialogue with God. No matter what it looks like, He delights in being with you. You will get more out of a few moments with Him than double the sleep you'd get in that time.

Standing firm looks like remembering our Father, prioritizing Him, and choosing to spend time with Him. He'll fill you with all you need for the day, including the love to offer to others. Take a seat with Him. Delight in the abundance of goodness and grace He offers day after day. As we spend more time with Him, we'll begin to resemble and reflect Him more and more. And no matter what each day brings, we'll find peace in unexpected places by remembering we've got all we need in our Father.

Chapter 17

RECOGNIZING PEACE

RECOGNIZING PEACE TAKES A TRAINED EYE. LIFE IS PRETTY GOOD at disguising peace. Our responses to what happens to us are often trained by the reactions we see others have. We may not realize that we're completely capable of handling everything that comes our way because we've got the King of creation in our corner. We don't need to have the natural reaction that the world would have because we may look at life a bit differently. Jesus offers the lens of peace through every circumstance.

During a tough workout, you might ask yourself, "How am I going to get through this?" For the most part, despite what you thought, you probably finish. Your body just keeps doing what it was built to do: breathing through it.

I was once doing a workout with my brother at a gym I was visiting. Lucky for him, it was a partner workout that went back and forth between running and rowing. It was a rough combination. We ran the four hundred meters together, and then we split the rowing to get to eighty-five calories. Every eleven calories I burned, we'd switch—and he'd get eighteen calories each turn. The running and rowing were rough because there wasn't much room for resting or catching our breath. We needed our heart rates to settle whenever they could. It always timed out in the rows that I was the last to go, and we'd jump straight into the run. My legs were burning, and my heart rate was going. I had to find rest in the run. I had to turn something that felt like full effort into a place I could make room to breathe and recover.

It took looking at the run differently. During the run, I had to protect my mind from negative self-talk about all the reasons I wouldn't make it. I had to look outside myself. I noticed how well my brother was doing in keeping up with the pace he wanted. I noticed the changing colors of the trees and made it around one corner at a time. We ran around a street block, and each turn would bring its own recovery and peace. Until then, I would just take it one breath at a time. I was filled with hope during that run because I saw it as a place of rest. Even when we're doing something difficult, if we focus on breathing through it, we can keep going when we don't think we can. Let breathing be a source of rest.

We can turn unexpected moments into places of rest or active recovery. We have to train ourselves to excuse the negative self-talk that tries to creep in. And we have to cover those challenging moments with hope by approaching them as places of rest. We're always capable of more than we think. Sometimes it's easy to ask ourselves how we feel about a moment instead of giving ourselves permission to just be present and experience it. No matter how difficult something is, we're always capable of breathing through it. We always have breath. When you feel like you're up against everything opposing peace, lean in and look for it. If you approach the unexpected places as places of rest, you might just find enough peace to take another breath and keep going.

HOMESICK

For a couple years, I lived about four hours from home. I definitely made it back more often than most people would have. I love home, and home is where my people are. As often as I went home, leaving never seemed to get easier. Home always felt like home, but leaving was always a pull between my heart and responsibility. Reluctantly, I always took the road of responsibility and went where I was called in that season. As I was leaving, I looked toward the next time I'd be home. I challenged myself to consider what a gift that season was living away from home, apart from my people. It was an opportunity to grow. I had definitely seen the downside of always trying to get home. I missed what was in the place I'd been called to. Where the Lord has you is not an accident. Going home as much as I did could have caused me to miss a whole bunch of what God had in mind to accomplish in that place. I saw home as fuel to press on, but maybe God saw it as a distraction.

I thought, *Thank goodness we can't go back and forth between heaven and earth while we're on assignment in this life.* We'd always try to get home and miss all that the Lord has brought us here to accomplish. We would want to spend all our time where we belong. Thank goodness we can't go back and forth. Nothing on this earth can satisfy, which confirms that this isn't our home. Each and every day is one step closer to our eternal home. Until then, we have to live our fullest life and our fullest purpose where our feet are.

During the first few months of the 2020 pandemic, I wrote a devotion that I've found still carries encouragement:

Here's to all the growth, grace, and new rhythms we've found in the unexpected unraveling of our norms and discovered that, even here, we're still OK. Even here, all the goodbyes, missing others, and growing pains made plenty of room for new hellos, becoming, and narrowing in on what matters and lasts.

This world is an easy place to watch the enemy instead of Jesus. It's an easy place to watch all the ways Satan has tattered and torn our calendars and expectations of our prayers, hopes, and dreams. When we're so fixated on the enemy, we miss all the hope and miracles Jesus fills in each purpose-packed trip around the sun.

The seasons that have seemed all too quiet are the ones that have enabled us to sift through our schedules and tame all the commotion of life. They may lead us to a point of uncomfortable stillness. Those are the ones that have given us the space to reevaluate all we stack our days, weeks, and months with and allowed us to reconsider what we continually run back to.

Between the deep sighs and exhales, this world will continually challenge our beliefs, behaviors, and comfort zones, but when the going gets tough, we get tougher. Even here, there is good if we're willing to be where our feet are and fight for it.

Here's to the moments, months, and years that chisel and shape who we are and who we're becoming and require each of us to actively choose, day after day, to make this version of life worth living. Even here, there is purpose. Even here, there is joy. Even here, there is hope. Even here, there is space to celebrate what has been and wait on the edge of our seats in eager anticipation for what will be. Even here.

The unexplainable aches and pains in life may just be the heartache of being homesick. You're getting there. Every day on this side of heaven is a gift to make the streets of gold crowded. We'll find peace in the midst of the heartache when we look for our Savior in it all. He's in the morning light. He's in the close calls, big breaks, warm cups of coffee, little smiles, and supernatural miracles. He's everywhere. He's in everything. If we look for Him, we'll find Him through and through. In those little glimpses of what's to come, we will find the hope and peace to take another breath and keep in step with the Spirit. Keep dreaming of home, but don't miss the life you've been entrusted with here and now. There's good here. There's peace here. Look for it.

THE INVITATION

If you've felt like there's a big stone wall between you and God, that's OK. I encourage you to consider what has stacked those stones. We all come from brokenness. That's why Jesus came. When did our world become so resistant to saving?

The brokenness of people can get in the way of seeing Jesus for who He is and the hope He has for us. Resisting His saving hurts us. We think we can make it through on our own, but our source of hope, joy, and peace are found in Him. There are millions of little miracles to catch, ponder, and treasure each day—if we look for them. It's easy to give the gifts credit for their goodness rather than giving the Giver of creation credit for the Creator's work. This world points a lot of fingers at where glory is due, and it's easy to get them all mixed up. Every day, we have a stack of invitations waiting for us, and they are all promising they're the key to happiness, hope, peace, or the answer to whatever challenge we're facing. We're constantly shuffling through the stack of the world's invitations to find which resonates with us most.

The world's invitations come in every form: careers, social status, friend groups, salaries, weight, and text messages. They come in extravagant packaging and simple packaging, but all of these invitations are only temporary. For a temporary amount of time or maybe even a season of life, they seem to satisfy what we're looking for. There is only one invitation that has no criteria or conditions. A relationship with Jesus comes every day forevermore, and it is everlasting. It is the only invitation that fully satisfies and invites you closer to the steps of heaven. We develop a habit of ignoring this invitation or even intentionally looking past it, thinking that it will come again. We lose the sense of urgency to receive and open the invitation. Maybe we're not interested because of a hurt we've experienced from people who had a relationship with God.

We are in a dangerous territory when we choose to check our options and receive other invitations. These other invitations might require something of you. They might cost you a piece of who you are. They might be a lesser version of the life Jesus is inviting you to. Nothing will compare to the invitation that comes from the kingdom of heaven. It's sealed with the blood of Jesus and signed "It is finished" by the One who took our place. This invitation was written by a Father who desperately wants us back in His arms. It's a letter of His love, His dreams for our lives, His plans, and a description of the place He is preparing for us. He watches us go through life, trying every invitation, as we shuffle His letter back to the bottom of the stack. He knows that we know He is what we need, but we are too reluctant and conditioned by the world to accept such love so freely.

It's easy to accept a love we think we deserve, but it's not as easy to accept a love we can't grasp. Jesus doesn't go where He isn't invited. He shakes the dust off His feet and keeps going. At the same time, His invitation still stands. He is hoping, pleading, and praying that you'll accept it someday. What if we did? What if we invited Him in?

Imagine your soul as a house. It's weathered some tough stuff. It's a creaky, run-down wooden shack with leaks in the roof, holes in the floor, and clutter and filth throughout. All the doors are locked and boarded up for protection against the hurts and heartache you're far too familiar with. You're just keeping yourself entertained, wandering through each day, and waiting for the next thing, which could finally be what you've been looking for. The next empty promise is sure to be different from the last. Then, in the midst of your waiting and wandering, you hear a knock. You peek out your window. A man dressed in white with wounds on His hands and feet knocks, stands, and waits. He makes His presence known, but you carry on. You keep yourself busy with all the wandering and searching you're doing within the locked and boarded walls. Maybe you'll dare to open the door someday—just at the thought of who this man on the other side could be.

Inviting Jesus in can be a whisper or the ache of your spirit—even behind locked and boarded doors. Maybe it starts with leaning your ear up against the door and listening to what He has to say. Maybe we can begin to deconstruct the barricades we've built between us and Him. The boarded-up doors will be taken down, nail by nail, as we remember His wounds that should have been ours. We unlock the rusted-shut lock and believe freedom is on the other side. On the other side of that door, we find the King.

Our boarded-up and locked souls are made up of aches, pains, lies, pride, shame, and the empty promises the world has tempted us with. All that's left us wounded and weary entered our lives as an invitation. We will find we're only in captivity by our own doing. We're carrying our own chains. What if we were willing to expose our broken souls to the Healer? The Restorer and King can minister directly to our deepest hurts. All these aches and longings we've gone to empty places to fix and fill have just been the longings for our King Jesus. We have been homesick for our heavenly home.

If any ounce of you is yearning for what could be on the other side of your locked and boarded-up door, lean your ear up against it. There is no need to clean up beforehand. He knows and treasures you as you are. Jesus's love and power are not limited by the barricades we build. If you allow yourself to receive the freedom and true life He has died for you to take, you will taste and see the hope, goodness, and healing of the eternal promises you've been looking and longing for.

Maybe today is the day you decide to crack open the door and see the outstretched, nail-pierced hand that is ready to lead you on a hope-filled, purpose-lined path home.

Chapter 18

SWIMSUIT SCARS

THERE ARE SOME THINGS IN LIFE THAT MAY BE PLACES OF DISCOMFORT, but you still have to take them on. Everything is uncomfortable at first, and as we do it more, we grow more comfortable. Some things might always be uncomfortable, and we have to learn to face those things boldly and bravely.

One of those uncomfortable things for me was the swimsuit competition for Miss Illinois. I jumped into the highest age division of competition at a local qualifying level rather quickly, and there was a lot of room for improvement. I've struggled with body image for a good bit of my life, and walking on stage in a swimsuit and heels to be judged for my body was terrifying. I knew I'd have to have a transformation mentally and physically to keep it from being my weakest phase of competition or even weigh down my score. I wouldn't allow there to be a weak link in the competition. I was there to compete. That was an area that I could have a lot of power over by how I presented myself. A drastic transformation was on the agenda.

I hired a trainer and nutritionist who I had worked with before. I knew she would get me where I needed to be, but she was tough. The schedule to a full transformation was intense. It was an extremely specific meal plan and two-a-day workouts six days a week. The mornings were fasted cardio on the stair climber and a sprint workout, and took between forty-five minutes to an hour and fifteen minutes. Later in the day, I had weightlifting workouts. On Mondays, I would send my trainer my weight and progress pictures. It was fun to have such a challenge each day and to have someone to hold me accountable.

The progress was real, but it had its ups and downs. It depended primarily on following the meal plan exactly. It was a difficult, exhausting journey, but I knew the end goal. I was able to handle the struggle because I knew the end result. I knew how I would look by that point was completely up to the effort I put in. I knew there would be a direct correlation. What I put in was what I would get out. Whenever I was tempted by treats, I'd think of the mission in mind and my end goal. Remembering both helped disarm temptation and allowed me to walk away in peace.

It's the same in life. We can struggle through anything if we know there's an end to the challenge. We can all suffer for a little while. We often get out what we put in. We reap what we sow. The physique was only a part of the battle when preparing for the swimsuit phase. An even more comprehensive aspect of swimsuit was learning to embrace, love, and celebrate my body. I wanted to learn how to genuinely love my body so I would be confident and proud when I competed.

During one of my training sessions for modeling in a swimsuit, someone who offered a lot of support and guidance came up to me while I was in my swimsuit. She grabbed some of my belly fat and told me it would keep me from winning. That lit a fire beneath my feet. That experience was one I did not enjoy in the moment. Even though that was a large offense to put on someone who has always struggled with body image, I chose not to pick it up. If something hurtful is placed in front of us, we don't have to carry it around. It's our choice. We don't need to tote that weight around. We can acknowledge it, forgive it, and leave it there. We can use it as fuel for change, and it might be the most powerful kind of fuel. It was for me.

As I was rebuilding my body, I changed how I saw my workouts. I quit asking myself how I felt about doing a workout and just did it—and the same with what my meals looked like. I needed a mental, emotional, and physical transformation to compete well. For Miss Illinois, I believed what I brought to each phase of competition was equal. My physical transformation was right where it needed to be. I had never been as proud of my body and the work I put in to transform it. When I took the stage, I felt such peace. Thanking my Creator for how He made me and reflecting on all the preparations paved the way for perfect peace. Throughout the process, I kept the end in mind, and it fueled my drive to accomplish what I had set out to.

Jesus is the ultimate example of this. He knew where He was going, and He knew how to get there. He knew His purpose and what He had set out to accomplish. Because He knew the end, He could endure the suffering. No matter what the suffering is for or from, we can make it too. Because of Jesus, we know the end. Let's pursue our purpose with the end goal in mind. In the midst of it all, we'll witness our Savior pave the way for perfect peace.

THE STRAY CAT

One of the toughest parts preparing for swimsuit was the nutrition aspect. It was very strict. I learned a lot about food, and I learned that what I ate was what I craved. You crave what you consume. If I ate almond butter, I wanted almond butter. My best approach for sticking to my nutrition plan was sticking to my nutrition plan. When I had cravings, I had a routine of drinking tea with a healthy sweetener. It was my way of diverting myself from cravings. I gave myself more of what I wanted to crave. I gave myself more of what would be good for me and not destructive to the purpose I had set out to accomplish. It is the same in life. Whatever we fill our minds with determines the wiring of our thought processes, and those thoughts will be the ones we crave.

What do we fill our minds with? The thoughts we feed will grow.

The enemy knows this about us, and he is very strategic about how he gets his foothold. He starts with something small—something we might think is OK to think about—and then he grows that thought. He tries to convince us that it's "just a little lie." He expands that belief to cover more ground. It's a slippery slope. The enemy knows when we are most vulnerable. He dangles the carrot at just the right time and in just the right place. He knows his targets and the places he plans every attack. We're not going to tolerate being the enemy's prey.

The enemy is like a stray cat. If we fall for what he tempts us with, we are feeding the stray cat. When a stray cat gets fed, it keeps going back to the spot where it found food. It begins to stick around, waiting for more, and it grows each time. Quit feeding the stray cat. You're only making it stronger. Don't let him feed on you. Our greatest protection is only consuming what we want to crave. The most powerful and effective thing we can consume is God's truth.

In His Word, He tells us to put on the full armor of God and suit up for battle. He is talking about the battle of temptation we'll face in the war zone of our minds. Prayer is our most powerful weapon against the enemy. It's the most productive thing we can do in the shortest amount of time, and it arms us with the power of the Holy Spirit. Prayer pushes back the kingdom of darkness. The enemy will have to bend his knee at the voice of prayer.

Let's pray hard and thank God for the war that's already been won by our Savior. Suit up for war. Make the stray cat flee. The enemy shakes in his boots at the thought of you. Let's make him crumble at the voice of prayer.

Broken Cisterns

One of the best things we can do for ourselves is learning to make the places of discomfort our wheelhouse. Let's run toward what intimidates us and cultivate peace within ourselves in those places. For some reason, I truly love doing this. I usually question my sanity at some point in the process of pursuing things that make me uncomfortable, like scuba diving, running a marathon, or backpacking.

During the backpacking experience at Beyond Malibu, we had an evening of preparation the night before beginning a route to a summit. While we were learning about what to expect in the week ahead, one of the guides shared something I still carry with me. She told us to imagine we were all cisterns (huge tanks that hold water). The week ahead would empty out everything in us, and it would take all of us to accomplish this feat, but that was the intent. In that week, we were meant to be emptied out so that all the filth on the bottom that had been stuck beneath the layers could be cleaned out. Maybe the cracks and leaks would be revealed so they could be repaired. In the highest highs and lowest lows of this experience, we would be filled back up to the point of overflow.

In order for us to be cleaned out, purified, and restored, we have to get to the dirt that's been stuck on the bottom and in the corners of who we are. It's been there so long that we might have forgotten it was there or not even noticed it. We have to be emptied out before we can scrub out what's been stuck on the bottom. It is not a comfortable process—no matter what it looks like—but we can endure anything when we know the purpose behind it.

We have to be careful not to fill our cisterns with anything but the Living Water. We will try to run to wells in this world that promise to offer something that will quench our thirst, but only the Living Water through our relationship with Jesus can do that.

At the toughest moments during that experience, we were able to endure because we knew there was a purpose to the pain. It was all part of what the Lord was doing with the cracks and corners of our hearts. Throughout our lives, we will have seasons that God will use to empty us out to clean and restore the cracks and corners of our hearts to make us more and more like His Son.

Once we're emptied and God's done His work to clean us out, let's guard our hearts carefully with what we fill it back up with: only

Jesus, only the Living Water. Through the ups and downs of life, know there is purpose to the pain. We're being cleaned out just to be filled to the point of overflow with what satisfies. Since we know the purpose, we can endure and find peace in the pain.

Chapter 19

SHOW UP

SOMETIMES THE TOUGHEST THING TO DO IS SHOW UP—WHETHER it is with God, another person, or yourself. All it takes is getting there, but that part seems to weigh on us the most. Prior to showing up, we weigh our options and what it requires and costs of us physically, mentally, and emotionally. We do this even with the good things in life. For some reason, we're quick to study the overall expenditure of something before we're willing to act on it.

Showing up looks different in every circumstance; whether it is through a text or a physical presence, it still counts. Consider the impact your presence could have. Your presence is seen and noticed, and it matters. Take up your space. Think of all we miss when we don't. When we feel the nudge to go somewhere and show up, the Lord has a holy hope in mind for us there. There's always more to lose by not showing up.

While writing this book, I often sat down without a whole lot to say. However, when I showed up and just started, the Lord always showed up—and so did the words. I'm completely unqualified, yet God put it on my heart to write. Once He entrusted me with putting words between two covers, it was my job to show up. It is the same with our moments with God. It's OK if you have nothing to say. It's OK if you don't know what to do in that space. The Lord will always show up where you do. He's faithful—even when we tend not to be.

Show up before you see the purpose or before you even know why. It'll be clear once you're there, and if it isn't, you're practicing more than you see when you show up. By showing up, you're practicing discipline, you're practicing courage, you're practicing intentionality, you're practicing love, and you're practicing the pursuit of purpose.

You develop what you practice. Let's exercise the muscle of intentionality and keep on showing up. As we grow more consistent and build this muscle, transformation begins to take place. A heart of intentionality will soon be your most natural posture.

My dad always says, "Don't deprive the world of who you are." The world needs you. You're not on assignment in this world to keep to yourself. Show up. We need you.

Missed My Final

I've had a few too many occurrences when I didn't show up, and it cost me a letter grade and a whole lot of tears. I forgot my final exam. I was a freshman in college, a very low season of life, and the class was the last thing on my mind. It was also online. For me, it was the perfect formula for forgetting an exam.

The worst part of the little miss was that I didn't realize it until four days after the final. During a two-hour time slot, a link was open for taking the final exam. However, it truly never crossed my mind until four days later. When I realized I had missed it, I began to panic. That was extremely out of character for me. I'm usually pretty on top of things that carry weight and importance. My to-do list is always in priority order.

I checked the link, and it was closed. I began to cry. I ran to my brother's dorm room and knocked on the door. I was sobbing. I told him what happened with every breath I could find—and he just laughed. He laughed a lot. He couldn't believe that I forgot it in the first place and then did not even notice for four days. We talked through what I should do and what it would do to my grade and my transcript.

I typed an email to the professor. Another unfortunate aspect was that the professor happened to be my academic counselor. After a carefully crafted email, I sent it. I got a rather quick response.

He just said he hoped it was a lesson for the future, and he welcomed me to college. Yikes! That is not how you want to kick off your higher education experience. It ended up giving my GPA and my transcript a bit of a rock, but I knew it would. I was pretty upset at myself for a while. It definitely spurred on a season that was filled with pretty rough self-talk. I thought about all the academic awards and internships I wouldn't get because of a hiccup in the first eight weeks of my freshman year of college. I did end up missing out on some academic achievements, but I learned a lot from it. I learned the importance of showing up and making room for grace. My brother helped me do that when I couldn't do it for myself.

It all begins with showing up. When we miss a moment that we shouldn't have, we should try to show up in the ways we still can. We can show up in humility, ready to learn and press on. We won't miss what God has in mind for our lives because of our inadequacy. We won't be robbed of His goodness because of all the places we fall short. If life were directly correlated to our performance of living life well, we'd all be in much different places. There's room for grace in every season. If it's not offered by the people around you, offer it to yourself and those who could use a bit more of it. You don't need to ponder what cannot be changed. Even when things aren't fair, we can control how we handle life. Let's not get fixated.

We all need grace at some point or another. I probably need a whole lot more than the average person. I bet God got a pretty good chuckle when my parents decided to name me Grace. He knew I'd need a lot of it. If I'm known for nothing else, I hope it's as a person who handed out grace like confetti. It's seemed like that's how God has freely given it to me. It's like it's waiting in places He knew I'd need it. I've been lined, filled, and covered with it by my Savior. I've needed every bit. We all do. Let's give grace like it's been given to us. Freely. Like confetti.

Let's show up for ourselves and for others. Let's be willing to sit with people in their messes and mistakes. Let's make room for grace if they can't for themselves. It's what we've already been freely given by a sweet and gracious Savior who has covered our inadequacies in His perfection. There's always room for grace—even after forgetting your first college final exam.

Two Left Shoes

I'm a triplet with two brothers. It's the best way to grow up. It's like growing up with your best friends. Growing up with your best friends means we do everything together, right? We sure did. One of those things was youth soccer, which was definitely not my cup of tea. It was a little too aggressive for me, but my brothers loved it. We all played on the same team.

For one game, one of my brothers couldn't make it that day. It was just two of us. We grabbed our matching cleats from the garage and jumped in the car. And as we were pulling up to the fields, I put on my cleats. It felt like my right foot had grown a whole bunch. It hardly fit in the cleat. I realized I had grabbed two left cleats. There was no way out of this one. I told my mom, but there wasn't time to go back. I shoved my right foot in that left cleat and showed up.

That was rough. It was the day of tripping. At the ripe age of eight, I learned I could play a soccer game with two left feet—and I'm a righty. By the end of that game, my feet and dignity were hurting, but I had showed up.

That day, I was taught the value of showing up with all you've got—even with two left cleats. When we're willing to show up with what we've got, we can do what we're there to do anyway. We can do it even when all the odds are stacked against us. We're capable of doing difficult things in unfortunate circumstances, and when we do, we expand our territory of peace.

Life depends on how we look at it. Take it as a challenge. Things don't need to go our way or be comfortable for us to be able to face them. Take life on exactly as things are; there is no need to wait for things to change. We're capable now—as we are. When we're willing to show up, just as we are, we find that we really do have a part to play. Your presence matters, and you might just find that the person next to you has two right cleats. It all starts with showing up.

PART 3
LIFE IS HOW YOU LOOK AT IT

Chapter 20

FOLLOW THE RECIPE

I LOVE TO BAKE. I LOVE IT. I THINK IT IS SO FUN AND SO THERAPEUTIC and rewarding with a fun sweet treat to share and enjoy as the end result. That being said, I am a horrible baker. We're talkin' bad. For a high school bake sale, I signed up to make cupcakes. I'm a big fan of cupcakes. I typically use a box mix to make most of what I bake, which honestly is even more embarrassing since I'm still as bad as I am.

I wanted to make a pretty decent amount for the bake sale, so I decided to triple the recipe. I put in my first box of cake mix and added triple the amount of oil and eggs and stirred it all up and began putting the batter in each cupcake liner in the tin. I filled about three cupcake pans as planned. I baked them, frosted them, put them in the fridge, and took them to the bake sale the next morning. We sold them for a dollar each at the fundraiser. The first couple sold, and then they began to sell fast. One guy kept coming back. The second time he came back, he was still finishing his first one. I noticed the cupcake was dripping, and I took another look at it. I quickly realized it was not normal. *What did I do? What did I put in these?*

I took a good, hard look at all the cupcakes in front of me and the line of people coming to buy them. I also took a good, hard look at the past twelve hours of my life—and what I did to the cupcakes to cause them to drip. And then it hit me—and it hit me hard. I had tripled all the ingredients except for the cupcake mix: triple the oil and triple the eggs, but only one box of cupcake mix. The cupcakes were dripping with all the oil, but they were clearly a hit. They were my best-selling cupcakes ever.

I'm bad at baking because I'm bad at following recipes. I'm a little too distracted when I'm in the kitchen, and I don't always recognize the importance of sticking with the instructions and formulas given to reach the results I've set out to achieve. I eye the measuring, and I level things out over the bowl. How we approach and follow the recipes will show itself in the results.

There's a formula for life too. It's the Bible, and the Holy Spirit is guiding every step to follow the formula. Only one person who has ever walked this planet can ever say they were good at following it, and that's Jesus. How we approach His Word will show itself in the ways we live. Our lives will likely be a direct reflection of how we follow our Father's formula. His ways were created out of love and are in place for our good. They protect us and ensure the very best for our lives. The closer we follow His formula, the more truth will fill our moments. Life will overflow with His peace when it's lined with His truth. Follow the formula; it's the way to peace and, in some cases, to a cupcake that won't drip.

First Pitch

Here's a palm-to-face moment and a good cringe laugh. A few months after winning Miss Illinois, I was asked to throw out the first pitch at a Major League Baseball game. I was honored, excited, and terrified. I started preparing about a month out; I called every athletic person I knew, including my brothers and my dad. I met with three coaches and one pitcher. By the end of their coaching and all the practice, I could throw a pretty solid pitch.

My prep team gave me a routine of what I should do before going out and throwing on game day. They broke down the mechanics and made everything very clear so I could ensure a good throw. We had a formula. I practiced my windup, my throw, and how I held the ball. I was ready, and I felt confident. *How hard can it be? Just throw the ball. Too easy.*

On game day, I put on my jersey. Since I needed to look the part of Miss Illinois, I wore my cutest wedges and white shorts. We were in the lounges by the dugout when they told me it was time to head out. I was waiting on the side of the field, and the weight of my nerves just slapped me in the face. I was terrified and forgot everything. To this day, I'm not sure I've ever been more nervous about anything.

They announced my name, and I walked up to the pitcher's mound. The pitcher gave me the ball, and the announcer did a play-by-play of my every move. My hands were shaky and sweaty. I glanced at the crowd, at the pitcher, and at my family—and then I took a breath. "Here's the windup and the pitch. Oh!"

I forgot to let go. I let go at the very end, and the ball spiked the ground about three feet to my left. Oh, boy. I shrugged and laughed, and the player ran up, handed me the ball, laughed, and ran off. It was so embarrassing. My windup looked good. It was solid, but the throw revealed my state of mind and showed that I hadn't practiced enough.

I walked off to a number of chuckles. My family was more in the palm-to-face mode. We went to the stands to watch the game, and throughout the time there, I'd get all sorts of passing comments about being "the chick who threw the first pitch." They even, graciously, replayed my first pitch in the sixth inning just in case anyone had missed it. Things had really gone south earlier in the day. First of all, I chose the wedges. They were cute, but I hadn't practiced in them. Secondly, I didn't practice under pressure. And third, I didn't remember the formula.

We have to remember the formula when we are under pressure, which takes practice. It takes a lot of practice. It requires knowing the formula, which is God's Word, enabling that truth to be second nature and a reflex under pressure. My formula for the first pitch was not anywhere close to second nature. In practice, I focused on every step. When the pressure hit, I forgot the formula. How often do we do this in life? When life hits, the truth we know from the Bible likely goes out the window. It means we need more practice with it. We need more practice being in the Bible, absorbing its truth, and living it out under pressure. Our windups may look good, but how we throw will reveal where we really are.

Let's practice God's formula by living it out, all the time, and not just in the moments we think mean something. How we live always means something. How we practice following His Word now, in our day-to-day lives, will reveal where we really are when the pressure hits. When we know the formula, His Word, we know peace. Remember the formula.

THE NATIONAL ANTHEM

I've clearly had my fair share of unfortunate moments when I didn't stick to the formula. Since I grew up as a dancer, dancing was my talent in pageants. During my time as Miss Illinois Teen, I was often asked to sing the National Anthem. After a couple polite declines, I finally gave in and said yes. Most of the requests were random events or pageants. The first couple were pageants. My second one was in front of some of my executive board members, a crowd I wanted to do well for. I practiced a lot. I met with a voice coach and my choir teacher, and we had a little pre-National Anthem routine I'd go through to be sure I was warmed up. My biggest concern was keeping my starting pitch since I performed a cappella.

Before walking out on the stage, I used an app to get my starting pitch one more time. I was announced, the audience stood, and the spotlight was on the flag and me. Once I began, I got the first couple verses down, and then I sang words I didn't mean to sing at that point in the song. I kept going and tried to find the right words in the right place. Cringe. That had never happened in any of my practices, and figuring out how to recover did not go too well. I eventually found the words and sang them in the right order. I definitely kicked off the show with some quality entertainment and a big yikes. While I was struggling, I almost just said, "Everybody, join me." As humorous as it would have been at that point, they all knew the words when I didn't—and they could have helped me.

In this case, the formula was the words, but I forgot them under pressure. We have to make the places of pressure our wheelhouse, but when we find ourselves forgetting the formula in a place and time when everyone around us knows the formula too, we can invite them to join in. Help yourself by making yourself available to be helped.

In the context of the formula being God's Word, community is a huge part of knowing and living out the Lord's truths. It's much easier when everyone around you is trying to do the same. When life gets heavy, and the pressure hits, invite others to join in. They will help us remember His truth, keep us on track, and point us in the direction of peace—and they might even help us remember the words to the National Anthem.

Chapter 21

PACKING PEACE

PEACE IS SOMETHING WE CAN CARRY. PEACE IS A GIFT AND A FRUIT of the Holy Spirit. When we know God, we know peace. While training for my marathon, I would often write words I wanted to remember or a Bible verse on my wrist before the run. During the run, I'd look down at it to remind me of my goal for that day. It helped me keep my mind on what mattered. Throughout the run, the writing would fade. By the end, it was usually hardly legible, but because I had studied the words throughout the run, I knew what they had said—even when they were no longer there. Since I studied the words and practiced the posture they inspired, by the end, I remembered the words and practiced that posture even when I couldn't see them.

It's the same with peace. When we've studied it and applied it enough throughout the good and the grind of life, we train our minds to remember what we've practiced—even when it can't seem to be found. That's when we dig and find that it's already within us by the work of the Holy Spirit. Those are the moments we can collect and remember when peace can't be found in our situation, season, or story. The more moments of peace we collect, the more we will carry. Then we'll begin to transform places that are desolate and disrupted with unrest and flood them with peace. That peace transcends understanding. That peace doesn't make sense. That peace is patchworked by the Holy Spirit and the moments we've collected and chosen to remember.

The ink on our arms will fade, and our faith can fade too. When that happens, reapply. Whether that is through writing it on your arm, going to church, reading the Bible, or growing in community, whatever that looks like for you, reapply. Reapply your faith so you can remember the truth that's bursting at the seams with the peace that transcends all understanding.

Let's practice peace now—in the good and the grind. Write the words that inspire the posture of peace and collect every moment peace brews. Study the words that stir it up and let its truth absorb. By the work of the Holy Spirit, peace will be an offering you carry wherever it lacks. Pack your peace and reapply. I think God delights in using people as vessels of His peace. His peace shows up when it doesn't make sense—in all the most unexpected places—because maybe it was carried there by someone who chose to remember it.

Miss Illinois Interview

In a lot of seasons in my life when peace didn't make itself obvious, I packed peace to carry with me to those places. One of those places was when I competed for Miss Illinois. Uncertainty can be a catalyst for anxiety. I packed peace. I paved the path ahead with prayer. When those moments I had prayed for arrived, there was perfect peace in moments when peace wouldn't have made sense and wouldn't have been naturally present.

One of the most fun but nerve-racking portions of competition for many people is interview. In the end, it carries the most weight in the competition. I prepared for the interview a lot. I did tons of mock interviews, and I studied current events and pop culture. I worked to understand the various sides of controversial subjects so I could know the why behind what I stood for. My mind had a running channel of reflective questions based on the world I was experiencing as I went about my day-to-day life. Once it was time to compete, I was ready. I didn't know what I was going to be asked, but I knew what I was going to say. I had a game plan.

I walked into interview, and the place I had prayed so earnestly for was paved with perfect peace. I was waiting to be hit by a wave of nerves, but I was at ease. The holiness and peace I had prayed for met me there. I had packed peace through prayer far before those moments came to pass. I could rest there in the midst of the moments that mattered most.

It was the toughest interview of my life. I was asked three consecutive questions that I truly didn't have an answer for. My answer for all three questions was the same: "I don't know."

By the third time, I jazzed up how I communicated that answer—but not by much. Those questions were specifically asking my thoughts on particular people in society. I should have probably known who they were, but I didn't. After those three tough questions, I was asked a question that I hadn't prepared for and didn't see coming.

I had given the head judge the impression that he and I were quite different in our beliefs and lifestyles. He asked me how, as Miss Illinois, I would relate to someone like him with such different belief systems and so many differences. I answered it honestly, and it's still an answer that, if asked again, would be the answer I believe I could improve upon for the rest of my life. I explained that no matter our differences and belief systems, we're all human. We can all relate at the most basic level of what we experience. We all know what trials and triumphs and inclusion and exclusion feel like. I would treat them the same as I would hope to be treated—with love and respect—regardless of our differences.

Throughout the interview, I tailored certain questions to fit the points and stories I wanted to communicate. Although that interview didn't go how I had planned or hoped, I felt peace throughout the entire thing. Hours after my interview, I truly wasn't sure how far I'd make it in the competition after that interview, but I felt peace.

That supernatural, perfect peace continued to show up in every moment of the competition. When I was standing in the final two, I felt perfect peace. That peace covered, filled and paved. There are no moments too small, too big, or too difficult for its power. This peace brews in prayer and is packable wherever we go. There is power in the way prayer increases our ability to pack peace. It's packing light and leaving the weight of worry behind. Packing light is packing peace—so pack light.

CROWD OUT WORRY

Peace is always packable, and it's always in our midst because it's a promise. Peace is a gift that comes with knowing Jesus. It always persists despite our circumstances and stands guard over our hearts and minds. There is truly nothing that can overpower peace because its source is Jesus. Peace is a gift.

For many of us, peace took up much more space in our minds as children. We weren't as good at welcoming worry. Maybe we have more to learn from little ones and the way they see life.

"What do you want to be when you grow up?" What was your response to this question when you were little? Let's say at four years old.

I wanted to be a veterinarian, a doctor, a dancer, a teacher, an author, a gymnast, a cashier, a designer, and a waitress.

What would you have said if someone had asked four-year-old you, "Who do you want to be when you grow up?" If someone were to ask you that same question now, what would you answer?

We always focus on the *what* and not necessarily on the *who*.

As we get older, the what clutters our minds with the worry of how we will reach what we believe we're supposed to be.

But that's always been the question: "*What* do you want to be when you grow up?"

They don't ask, "*Who* do you want to be when you grow up?"

I believe we never grow out of either question, but there is a difference. *What* puts the emphasis on a title, role, and position. *Who* puts the emphasis on who you are as a person, your character, and who you're becoming. We never grow out of becoming. That's something we'll always do.

We should always ask ourselves, "Who do you want to be when you grow up?"

I hope my answer now would be "Like Jesus: encompassing the fruits of the Spirit. Someone of love, joy, peace, forbearance, patience, kindness, goodness, faithfulness, gentleness, and self-control. I have a long, long way to go."

Every day we're becoming who we will be, but it's up to us to decide who we want to be. We still have work to do on shifting our focus. Maybe kids are better at *being* rather than *doing*. Maybe the shift comes from focusing less on the productivity to achieve our *what* and just delighting in being and naturally becoming and developing the *who*.

As we get older, we seem to tie the correlation of productivity and meaning tighter and tighter. Let this give you some room to breathe—even if something doesn't seem productive doesn't mean it's not meaningful. Most kids aren't as focused on their to-do lists as they are being kids and having fun. Their focus isn't on what they're becoming; they are just focused on being right where their feet are. What if we learned to do this too?

Let's crowd out worry by just being present right where we are. Little ones are so focused on the reality in front of them that they can't be distracted by the worries outside of that moment. They don't bother borrowing worry or weight from moments outside of the one they're in. Peace is always packed. It's light and easy. Let's live more like little ones and be less consumed about what we're becoming. Let's start packing peace and having fun again.

Chapter 22

THE SWEET SPOT OF OUR PURPOSE

AN INTERESTING ASPECT ABOUT MISS AMERICA IS THAT YOU MEET an individual from every state. This, of course, welcomes a wide array of differences—climate, culture, dialect, accents, beliefs, terrain, and traditions—all gathered in one place for a singular purpose. Despite our differences, we shared a common goal. We were all there to represent where we called home. Our differences didn't divide us because we had one goal in mind, and it transcended the boundaries our differences could have drawn. Instead, outside of our common goals, our differences united us. It was so interesting to learn about where each person came from, how they got there, and a bit about their story. We wanted to learn what composed each individual.

When we're willing to lean in when we're tempted to lean away, we discover just how much we have in common. Despite our differences, we could all relate emotionally throughout the week. There were moments of stress and moments of nerves and excitement and intensity, but we could all relate because of the feelings the experience brewed.

Since I was nervous before the competition each night, I'd asked my first and closest friend there, Miss South Dakota, if she wanted to pray. Each night, we held hands, bowed our heads, and prayed. This routine did not change between nights, but whose hands I held did. The first night was just Miss South Dakota and me, and with each night, more hands were added to the circle.

On finals night, almost every single contestant was there along with most of the hostesses in the dressing room, all circled up and holding hands. To this day, one of my greatest honors was getting to gather together with those women and bow our heads and come before our Savior on the brink of our biggest dream. What a sweet moment that was. Despite all the differences that could have divided us, we stood, hand in hand, and came before our Savior together.

Those who stayed on the outside of the circle were watching and listening closely. Maybe it was their first encounter with faith, hope, and a belief in something bigger. It was sweeter than any dream could ever be. Maybe it was their first access point to Jesus. What an honor it was to offer exposure to the Cornerstone, the One who changes everything.

I vividly remember opening my eyes to see those few on the outside of the circle as they stood close and watched closer. Maybe they were brimming with curiosity about this faith we all found hope in. The Savior we gathered before that night is the same Savior who meets us in the quietest moments of life. He is making my fingers dance along these letters that make up this book. He is steady and faithful.

While talking with our heavenly Father in such a nerve-racking moment, there was peace to be found. I felt like that moment was the entire reason I was there. Every moment had been orchestrated to reach that moment. We bowed our heads, held hands with strangers and sisters, and gathered before the King. That was the sweet spot of my purpose. When I stepped into the sweet spot of my purpose, even in the most nerve-racking moment, I found peace.

That experience was a glimpse into what being an access point can look like. Despite the differences that could have divided us, we were unified by what we had in common. Maybe we're all in the same boat a little more often than we think—if we choose to look for what unifies us rather than what divides us. Even loaded with differences, we can still stand hand in hand before Jesus. We can still be an access point to those watching closely from the outside and looking in. We don't need to go to Miss America to put this into practice. We can practice being an access point, loving the person beside us, and coming together before our Savior in the moments between the milestones. Let's look for the common ground or—better yet—create it. Let's be the access point and lean into the sweet spot of our purpose. That's how we can find peace in unexpected places.

SEASONS

My favorite season is fall. I love the weather, and I love the anticipation of the holidays. I love the leaves and the evidence of changing seasons when the leaves turn color. One fall, I was walking after a lot of the leaves had fallen. The path was covered with leaves. I was slowly shuffling through the layers beneath my feet, and each leaf was so different. The shapes, the sizes, the textures, the colors, and the veins were all unique. Their differences indicated where they came from. One singular leaf can indicate whether a leaf came from an oak, an elm, or a sugar maple—and everything in between. The shapes, sizes, textures, colors, and veins are all clues into their roots.

Oaks feed migrating birds with their acorns. Elms are often valuable homes for animals. Sugar maples are valued for furniture, flooring, and instruments. With more than sixty thousand tree species all around the world, each is created to serve a unique purpose. Every single one is needed, intentionally designed, uniquely beautiful, and designed to fulfill a purpose. Their differences reveal their value.

Let's put this in terms of people. There are close to eight billion people in the world, and all of them were created uniquely and designed to serve a specific purpose. Each and every one is needed, intentionally designed, uniquely beautiful, and designed to fulfill a purpose. Let's learn to stroll through life and admire the layers of beauty all around us. Let's embrace the differences and varying purposes that we all have to offer.

Let's admire the beauty and purpose of others without questioning our own, knowing that what we have to offer is uniquely needed and valuable too. May the way we live and act and speak be a clear indication that we are not of this world; we are followers of Jesus and citizens of heaven. Our differences do not negate our beauty; they enhance it. Our differences reveal our value and the need for each and every soul. There's so much to learn from nature. I think that's how God intended it. It is not for creation to get the glory; it is for creation to point to the Creator. When we're able to wrap our minds around the value and beauty that our distinctive qualities offer, we can begin to live in the sweet spot of our purpose.

THE SAME GOD

The God who was with us in those moments before finals night at Miss America—or taking a stroll on an ordinary fall day through a path piled with leaves—is also with us now. The same God who enabled our first heartbeat has been the same faithful Father through every season. He has been steady in the moments and the milestones. The God who knit us together while we were hidden yet known is the same God who crafted this day. He knew every day before one of them came to be.

When God was dreaming up who we'd become, He knew how He'd help us get there. He knew the ups and downs, the twists and turns, and the forks in the road we'd navigate. It's always been Him. He's never changed. He was with us when we opened our eyes for the first time in this world, our first steps, our first birthday, our first day of school, our first night living away from home, our first love, our first heartbreak, the first time we had to say goodbye to someone we loved, our greatest disappointments, and our sweetest milestones. He has always been there. He's with us in our day-to-day lives, in the mundane routines, in our stacked schedules, and in the in-between moments. He's here. It's Him, and it always will be. He will be with us in our last days too: our last job, our last Christmas, our last birthday, our last days living independently, the heaviest day when we say goodbye to our last and longest love, our last morning waking up on this side of heaven, and down to our last breath. He'll always be there. It's always been Him, and it always will be.

And when we've experienced the firsts and lasts on this earth, we'll wake up to the sound of trumpets and streets of gold. You'll come face-to-face with the same God who was with you through every first and last. The voice we've grown so familiar with will be matched with the face our hearts have ached for all our days. The One who knit us together, designated and designed us with a purpose that we were created to fulfill and equipped us with the Advocate, the Holy Spirit, to guide us to the sweet spot of our purpose every day.

Someday, we'll be home, welcomed to forever by the same God who is with us now. Until then, don't miss this moment. Lean in and live out the sweet spot of your purpose. Look for the One who never changes. It has always been Him, and it will always be Him.

Chapter 23

PURPOSE TO THE PROCESS

ONE THING I'VE ALWAYS ADMIRED ABOUT MY MOM IS HER ABILITY to DIY things. Whether it is repurposing or building furniture, designing and creating signs, building cardboard castles, or laying shiplap on a wall, she's always had the patience to figure things out. Her success rate is high—and she eventually figures things out—because she doesn't cut corners, and she takes every failure as another way not to do something. She isn't afraid of the process.

She and I attempted to renovate my childhood room. We had a vision of a beautiful oatmeal and white room with one wall accented with shiplap, and we dove right in. We picked the colors, laid down a painting tarp, and got rolling. We decided to shiplap a wall underneath a border. She had done some homework that I skipped out on, and she told me to gather a few quarters and pack my patience. We had a hammer and nails ready to go along with a bunch of quarters and carefully sized wooden slats.

We put the first wooden slat in the bottom corner of the wall and nailed it in, and then we brought out the quarters. We put down the next piece of wood beside the first one, and we put two quarters between them. I questioned the need for the quarters and insisted it would look fine and go much faster without that step.

My mom insisted that we keep with the quarter process, and we did. After hours and hours, we took a break. The process continued for a few days. Quarter by quarter and wooden slat by wooden slat, I was convinced there was no point for that level of accuracy. However, as she insisted, we kept the quarters in the process. Although it took some time, it was sweet to be sitting on the floor next to my mama as we created something together. We got to trust the process together, and once we finished and stepped back to look at what we had built, I realized how important the quarters were to the process. They had kept the spacing even and consistent.

There's always purpose to the process. Someday we'll understand—even if we don't at the moment. Trust the process. It's always easier to trust the process with people. Everything that seems mundane—or maybe even pointless—has a purpose, and there's more intention in the details of our lives than we may care to believe. Everything in your life is there with intention, and maybe only God knows why at this point. Things may be in place as a tool of refinement or a vessel for impact. Trust the process, lean into Jesus, stick with it, and someday you'll see. While you're waiting, gather a community to wait it out. There's purpose to the process; this might be part of your refinement to becoming more like our Savior.

Read the Instructions

I'm very bad at reading instructions. I am embarrassingly bad and pull on a door a couple times before I notice the bold letters at eye level reading "push." At some point in life, I became convinced that everything I would need to be able to do could be done without instructions. Everything could be obvious enough to figure out. The entire point of instructions is to instruct you in how to do or use things. I have countless examples of memorable moments from my lack of reading or following instructions.

One of the many things I've been told to read is my car owner's manual. I know the basics of making my car function. I can turn it on, take it from place to place, take it on some decently long road trips, and adjust the mirrors and seats. I also know how to connect my phone to the car.

I'm quite confident that I know the basics, but I have plenty of areas where I lack in knowing the full function of my vehicle. I'm not sure I could say I know what all the lights that come on are indicating. I don't know what every button or control does. However, if I were to ask the creator of the vehicle how to use it, they would be able to tell me every single detail. They would be able to tell me about every bell and whistle, how they were intended to be used and cared for, and all the car is capable of doing. The creator would know what every light indicates and how to discern when something needs care. The creator would know the intention behind each of its capabilities, all serving a purpose of safety, function, or comfort. The creator knows better than anyone how something is intended to be used to its full capacity.

I know very little about how to make my car function to its full capacity because I haven't read the owner's manual. The basic instructions explain how to use the vehicle correctly. I think we've gotten a whole lot wrong in this world from not reading, following, or knowing the instructions. We can't use something to its full potential—or even know how it was intended to be used—without knowing, reading, and following the instructions.

So many of us miss the mark on reading, knowing, or following the instructions we have been given for how to live this life. The Bible is our instruction manual. Since God knew we would struggle with this, He gave us the perfect example in His Son and the Holy Spirit. When we study the Bible, we learn the instructions, the indicators that something's not right, and how to discern when something in our lives needs care.

The Creator's instructions and wisdom are in place for our protection and best interests. They help us become more and more like Jesus. Let's study the instruction manual, God's Word, a bit more to learn how this life is supposed to be lived: fully and well. It's written to give us life and life to the full. In His Word, we can find peace like never before and the purpose we've been looking for our whole lives.

DISCERNING DISTRACTION

Writing this book has been a true joy, but as I've progressed, I've used snacks as little incentives and rewards. If I get too focused, I forget about the little rewards along the way. I forget that I was even hungry. I think that's what purpose does. It keeps us focused. Purpose is the best defense against distraction. When we're so captivated by purpose, we don't notice the distractions.

It can be difficult to discern a distraction. Purpose is a road with many twists and turns. I think it's easy to associate purpose with productivity, but I don't think they're always correlated. Things can be purposeful without being productive. Just because something isn't productive doesn't mean there isn't meaning and purpose behind it.

Those random inklings to reach out to someone or feelings that you're supposed to talk to someone—even strangers—are not accidents. When we know God, we've got the Holy Spirit in our ears. He is guiding us to live out our purpose. Jesus knew His purpose, and He knew how to discern distractions well. Mark 5 gives a glimpse into the life Jesus had and the things and people that were constantly pulling Him in every direction. The quality He mastered perfectly is discernment. He knew what needed His attention and the value of prioritizing some things over others. He knew what to pay closest attention to.

Jesus crossed over by boat, and a large crowd gathered around Him. It was a perfect opportunity to speak the truth to all who had gathered to listen, but a synagogue leader came up to Jesus and begged Him to put His hands on his dying daughter. This man could have been seen as a distraction. He was pulling Jesus away from the crowd, but Jesus discerned this man was the priority— and the crowds were the distraction. As Jesus was on His way to heal the synagogue leader's dying daughter, a woman reached out and touched the hem of His robe. He realized power had gone out of Him.

In the urgency of a dying child, Jesus stopped amid the crowds pressing in on Him. He was looking for the one who had touched the hem of His robe. It was a woman who had been bleeding for twelve years, and she had spent all she had on her search for healing. She believed, in faith, that she would be healed if she touched His clothes.

In the chaos of all the callings, He discerned that this woman was the priority and not the distraction. As He continued to the home of the dying child, they got news that the child had died. Jesus told them to not be afraid and to just believe. As He entered the house of mourning family and friends, He had everyone leave the room except for the child's parents and His disciples. He went to the child, took her hand, and told her to get up.

She immediately got up and began to walk around.

Jesus has mastered the valuable and precious quality of discerning distraction and recognizing what is truly important in each moment. His truth and spirit will guide us in this discernment as we continue to earnestly pursue a relationship with Him. Let's consider what we believe to be the distractions; are they really the distractions or are they moments that truly matter?

Some of our biggest distractions come from screens and scrolling. Our best defense is being captivated by purpose. As we begin to recognize the purpose in the process, read and know our Father's instructions, and discern distraction with eternally focused hearts, He will guide us into the sweet spot of our purpose.

Chapter 24

EQUIPPED AND QUALIFIED

YOU ARE MORE POWERFUL THAN YOU WILL EVER BELIEVE. YOU'RE locked and loaded with purpose. You are equipped and qualified. You can realize your power in the least expected moments.

I loved watching little Mozie Bear experience things for the first time as a puppy. She's a powerhouse pup. She loves to get into new things. Mozie likes to believe she is very independent and capable of taking things into her own paws. Her big thing is having access to everything. This world is hers; we're all just living in it.

One evening, I was in my room. I had closed my door enough for there to just be a slight crack in the door. She was napping in the living room. She noticed I had left the room, and she set out to find me. Once she realized where I was, she stood up on her hind legs and pushed the door open with her two front paws. She jumped down once the door started to move. Her front paws hit the ground hard, and she looked at me and back at the door, which had moved a couple inches. Although the door was plenty open for her to creep through, she went back on her hind legs, put her front paws back on the door, and pushed it open more. Her paws hit the floor again, and she looked back at me and back at the door. She didn't know she could do that. She didn't know she was that powerful. Mozie Bear was looking at me to affirm that she had done what she didn't know she could do.

I think we're all a little like that. We don't know our power until we do something we didn't know we could do or didn't think we could do. We'll often learn about our power in the moments we least expect it. If only you knew what you are capable of. If only you believed what you are capable of—enough to even try. You are equipped and qualified to do what you've been called to do.

Little Mozie Bear didn't know her power until she put it to the test. When we have enough faith to try, we can discover our power in our purpose—while being met with the affirmation of sweet peace in the moments we least expect it.

LEADING YOUNG LIFE

There were so many moments when I felt unqualified for the conversations I was entrusted with as a Young Life leader. The weight of what was shared—and the wear and tear those words had had on the individuals who had spoken them—were something I didn't know what to do with. I didn't have the right words or a solution. Most of the time, all I had to offer was a presence.

It was an honor to be entrusted with the reality of the individuals I got to love on as a leader. It's a privilege to get to share another's burdens and release a little built-up pressure in a safe place where true realities could be spoken. It was tough stuff. Real stuff. Stuff that would leave its mark on their stories.

I could hear every detail and offer a consistent presence time and time again, but I couldn't change their realities. However, I could offer the most powerful alternative. I could pray for them. It was the most powerful and effective thing I could offer. I could go before the Lord on their behalf and intercede for them. I could remember them in prayer. I could sit with them in the hurt and share in their burdens. I could affirm them and remind them that they were not fighting this fight alone. Regardless of how heavy and difficult the battle may seem, the war has already been won. It's an honor to be welcomed into the safe space of someone who is hurting.

We all are hurting in some way or another. Some people keep their safe spaces boarded up and locked away from the rest of the world. Maybe they are afraid of letting someone come close enough and hurting them again. Some may have more of an open door because they've learned that some people can enhance the safety of a space and offer support. Everyone approaches their hurts and hallelujahs differently, and that's OK. That's a good thing. It sure makes me unqualified for just about every situation I got to lean into with the kids I was leading. No story was the same, and neither was my approach or presence. It was whatever it needed to be, and we learned over time. For some, an arm's length was plenty close; for others, there was no limit on sleepovers, road trips, and girl talk.

I kind of loved being completely unqualified. It created plenty of space for the evident love, guidance, and power of the Lord to show up where I couldn't. It made room for Jesus to do His own dance. He and I were witnesses, and He picked up my slack. I tend to keep our heavenly Father pretty busy.

I'd imagine some doctors feel unqualified a good bit. Despite their countless hours and years of training, every case is different. The more the patient tells the doctor, the more they know how to minister to their needs and help them heal. If a patient were to just say they don't feel well, the doctor would work to narrow in on the specifics and find the root of the problem to treat it accordingly.

We have to do the same thing with the Lord. In all the moments we feel unqualified, and every moment in between, let's tell God about the specifics so He can minister to them directly. He already knows your needs, but He delights in the surrender offered in the invitation to His ministry. That is when we can be still and watch Him do what only He can do. In our stillness, He demonstrates His great resurrection power.

Leading Young Life will always be one of my greatest joys. I didn't know I'd be in as many of those situations, sharing in some heavy stuff, but the Lord did. I didn't believe I was equipped and qualified, but the Lord did. Where I wasn't equipped and qualified, He was. No matter what moments stir your feelings of inadequacy, invite the Lord to show up where you can't. Make room for Him to do what only He can. Be still, wait on His power, and just watch. Tell Him all the specifics so He can minister to you and your situation in every way He sees fit. By His grace and Holy Spirit, you can be transformed into the image of His Son. When we don't make the cut, but we make room for Jesus, we can find peace in unexpected places and purpose where we didn't think we had any.

Finding the Why

I try to make sense of a lot of my life through my understanding of my purpose in each specific season. Seasons change—and so do our roles and purposes. When we have Jesus, we're enabled to be flexible and dynamic with what that role and purpose is from season to season. Titles and routines will come and go.

In my life, in every season, I've questioned or wondered about a role or purpose. I always think about why the Lord has led me there, which often revealed my purpose in that place. That thought process has helped me make sense of most of my life. The other sweet aspect I've discovered in that approach is knowing that my why and my purpose can disarm the obstacles that could slow my impact. Those obstacles often look like comparing, impressing, or judging. Nothing good. When we're focused on understanding our purpose enough to understand it's an eternal assignment, we aren't as easily distracted.

When working to understand my eternal assignment in places and seasons, thinking about why I was there helped me narrow in on my purpose. In some seasons, I've found my eternal assignment has been to pray for those around me and intercede for them. If I didn't, who would? It tacked an urgency to my purpose in that place.

That urgency dealt with someone else's forever. I can't even begin to explain how often I've fallen short of the tasks entrusted to me. I was often distracted by things that didn't matter. When we are on the brink of being in the sweet spot of our purpose, the enemy knows. He prowls at your door. He knows the threat you are to his power and his plans.

A primary point to my presence throughout every season has always been prayer. I believe the Lord is up to something in the lives of those around us, and our prayers may be a special part of the process. Moses interceded for the people God wanted to destroy, and God listened to him. That's the power of prayer! God bends down to listen, and He delights in talking with His kids. Prayer releases God's power over people and situations. It welcomes God's power to enable and qualify every place that is lacking. Prayer may help us recognize our power in moments we didn't realize.

Revelation talks about golden bowls that the angels hold. They are full of the prayers of God's people. Let's fill those bowls to the point of overflow. Let's make them so heavy that they just pour over those we intercede for—and maybe they will begin to see the hope and life that are found in our Savior.

Chapter 25

IMPACT

PRAYER IS THE MOST POWERFUL AND EFFECTIVE WAY FOR IMPACT. However, there may be moments when our bravery is called into action. A sweet woman I met for a glimpse taught me that. Let me tell you about Rosemary.

On a Thursday morning, I arrived at the Charlotte airport at eight o'clock, but I was not renting a car until three o'clock. I found a cute, white rocking chair to park in most of the day to people watch and work through my to-do list. About four hours in, and I had already had many rocking chair neighbors. Some shared brief words, others shared none, and one shared many.

One rocking chair neighbor and I exchanged stories, hearts, and our dreams about eternity. This woman of wisdom sat in the rocking chair next to me and began commenting here and there. We eventually engaged in a conversation. She asked where I was headed, and I told her about Young Life—specifically the mission of Young Life—and even a little glimpse of the Gospel.

She asked more questions about my faith and added that she also loved Jesus. Her name was Rosemary. Rosemary began to unfold her story with tears. She had cancer, and her husband had survived what should have been a fatal car accident. She shared that these unbelievably horrible things were the very things that showed her how real and good our God is. Rosemary told me that she had sat next to me to share the Gospel. What boldness! It seemed so easy and natural. Her long layover led her to a faithful prayer: "God, use me in these hours of waiting." She invited Jesus to be her hands and feet in that airport. She had gone around sharing the Gospel and handing out little Bibles. She was talking to people and delighting in their stories, leaning in, listening, and sharing her own joys and hurts. She shared the reality and goodness of our Savior and the hope of forever. After our long, sweet conversation, which was clearly divinely orchestrated, she parted by saying, "I'll see you in heaven."

Who is your rocking chair neighbor? Who have you sat next to? Who has sat next to you? Every neighbor beside you is an opportunity and maybe even a divine appointment. Lean in and engage. Speak the truth in love. Love always has more to give. Maybe God is using these moments to change someone else's life forever and point them toward their purpose. Rosemary is after our Savior's heart with bravery and boldness. Let's spur on more conversations like Rosemary and carry on that bravery and boldness. May this be our prayer: "God, use me in these hours of waiting."

Let's make heaven crowded.

THE LADY IN BUSAN

I grew up traveling a good bit because my dad ran a travel company. One trip was traveling throughout Asia. We got to stop in Busan, South Korea. We visited the fish markets and wandered our way through the city, exploring all we could. We always tried to see enough of the nooks and crannies of a community to get a taste of what their day-to-day lives looked like. We wandered through the alleys with tucked away livelihoods, built on family businesses, soaking up space wherever they could.

As we wandered through one of the back streets, a woman who clearly had decades of wisdom, began to speak to me in Korean.

Although I didn't know what she was saying, she was warm and sweet. Behind her was a huge stand full of hazelnuts. She was selling them, and she was proud. She was filled with delight. After she realized I couldn't understand what she was saying, she took my hand with her small, dainty, worn hands and placed a hazelnut inside.

At first, I didn't know what it was. I looked at it closely and wondered what I was supposed to do with it. When I looked back at her, she grabbed another hazelnut and showed me how to peel it and bite into it. She handed it to me, and I tried it. She was right. It was a neat flavor, but her pride in what she was showing me spurred my interest. She held her chin high as she sold her hazelnuts. She believed in their value and believed she had a lot to offer. This belief in what she had inspired her bravery in what she did.

What if it was the same for us? What if we believed in something so much we couldn't keep it to ourselves? What if our belief in what we had inspired our bravery for what we did? When we know Jesus, we know how much of a cornerstone He is. He changes everything. Every heartbeat on this earth has the greatest gift of all time, a gift that changes forever. The gift of grace from our Savior is available to them. Let's not keep it to ourselves. We have something to offer that everyone needs and is looking for—whether or not they realize it. What if we had such faith in the power of Jesus that our belief in what we know inspired our bravery for what we do. We've got a lot to learn from this sweet old lady from Busan. Hazelnuts fueled her bravery—let our Savior fuel ours.

FACES IN THE FISH MARKET

Most of our time in Busan was spent moseying through the fish market. We were curious about the lifestyle of those who gathered their income from their street stands. The market was filled to the brim with vendors. Each one had something to offer and believed what they had carried value that visitors would invest in. Stands were stacked on top of each other. Some stands were more sophisticated than others. Some were little stools with makeshift tables holding things they had carved. Every individual had something to offer, and each person believed they belonged and showed up believing that day after day. They believed that what they offered held enough value to support their livelihood.

The faces of the fish market all had something in common. All their eyes were down. They were so focused on their work that they only looked up to serve customers. The sounds were so distinct to their roles and purposes there. There was a rhythm to the sound of one man's knife cutting off the heads of fish as they were cleaned. One after another, the same cuts with the same space of time between each chop made for a melody of his purpose. He believed the purpose he served there was urgent. His eyes were fixed on the task in front of him, and outsiders like me could hear the rhythm of his purpose through the steady work of his knife. The same applied to the man meticulously carving little wooden figures to sell. You could hear his knife peeling off little slices of wood to create something, and only he knew what it would become. You could hear the stamp maker carefully turn the handle on a little box to create little stamps. You could hear the knife maker sharpen each knife to perfection and smooth the handle with a grip that would appeal to any potential buyer.

Every individual there—no matter how similar their role looked to the people next to them—showed up believing and working as if they were the only one on earth who had what they offered. They believed something would come of the work of their hands and the consistency of their presence. They believed in their abilities and value of being there. They were brave in who they believed they were and their purpose in that place.

Let's learn from the faces in the fish market. They've found peace in unexpected places because of their pursuit of purpose, and we can too. Let's keep our eyes steady on the task at hand. Let's be so focused that others can hear the rhythm of our purpose. Let's show up day after day and believe that what we have to offer carries irreplaceable value. Let's be brave in who we are and the purpose we have in this place.

Chapter 26

ETERNAL ASSIGNMENT

THE SWEET THING ABOUT KNOWING AND TRUSTING JESUS IS THAT we never have to worry about if we're in the right place. If we're working to follow His lead through His Word, we can have confidence that we're exactly where we're supposed to be. In every space we're placed in and on the paths in between, let's bring the gifts and peace we've been entrusted with into that place.

What you offer may be a clue to why you're there. The qualities God anointed you with were given to accomplish the eternal assignment He's given you. The assignments might look different, but your role is the same. You must embrace the qualities you've been given to fulfill your purpose in that place. Don't water down who you are to blend in with your environment. You were placed there because of the qualities that set you apart. Our abilities, boldness, and bravery to be different can influence our level of impact. God doesn't give us a spirit of insecurity or fear. He gives us the bravery and peace to step into the full capacity of the qualities He's given us to impact. He's gone the distance to put just the right people in just the right places to receive the impact you can offer.

Throughout my life, whether it was showing up to dance rehearsals growing up, going to school or the grocery store, walking across the Miss America stage, or working as a lifestyle host, my role has been to impact the people around me. Impact happens through the power of prayer and the qualities God has intentionally and carefully tuned in our DNA.

Every day, we put on some sort of face. It could be a literal face of makeup or a face to take on the day. We become what and who we need to be to make it through the day. As we put on that face, let's remember who we were created to be and not let that get lost in the layers. Let's remember why we're there and load up on the hope and joy that we get to live out a day that God has packed with purpose.

As we practice this mentality of an urgent drive to pursue our purpose, we'll find that our what-ifs fade. When I first got a job as a TV lifestyle show host, I was certain they had the wrong girl. I was convinced they didn't realize I was fresh out of college, with little to no on-air experience. I was sure they would let me go once they realized who they had actually hired. The most basic things we use in TV every day are a mic and an IFB (to hear the control room). I didn't know how to put on either of them. All my worries and the insecurities that weighed on those moments of figuring out how to put those two things on every day faded as I practiced.

It's like working out. When you exercise a muscle, it is strengthened over time. Let's notice what aspects of our lives could use a little more work and focus on strengthening those areas and replacing the insecurities with impact. Keep pressing on in your purpose.

LIFELONG DREAMS

One thing I dreamed of a lot growing up was getting married. I'm not sure where this dream came from—maybe my parents. I had so many hopes, prayers, and dreams about who my husband would be. He would be gentle, kind, loving, caring, protective, loyal, strong, and intentional. He would delight in our heavenly Father and our family. I dreamed of who this man would be from a very young age.

Every year, beginning when I was two years old, my dad would take me to a daddy-daughter dance. He still tells me stories about them. After he asked me to my first daddy-daughter dance, I said two words: "Need dress." I took my ticket everywhere in the weeks leading up to the dance. I adored my dad, and that adoration has only grown since.

A few years later, at about the age of five, we were driving home from our annual daddy-daughter dance. As I was looking out the window from my car seat, my head was resting on the seat belt. I said, "Daddy, I don't ever want to leave you and Mommy, but I guess someday I'll find someone." I've dreamed of the man who would love me, the man I'd get to love all my days, for most of my life. I know I didn't plant this dream in my heart as a five-year-old, but I believe the Lord did.

As I got older, I wanted to remember that my husband, no matter how amazing, would never be my savior. Only Jesus can ever be my Savior. I believe the Lord places desires in our hearts to recognize every good gift, including your person, will come from Him and Him alone. Nothing comes from your doing.

In my early twenties, I decided that I wanted to run a marathon and write a book before I got married. I wanted to know I could do hard things all by myself. I wanted to instill deeply that I didn't need another person to impact people in the name of Jesus and fulfill my purpose. The Lord created me with the ability to live fully and completely with my own two feet. That being said, God didn't create us to be alone. Maybe another person can propel your purpose as you set out to love God and love people together. If you're in a time of being alone, our Father is most careful with you. He is faithful and with you and for you.

Let's remember where the dreams we have—and even the ones we're living out now—came from. If we're still waiting for our someday, someone, and every other dream to come around, we are valuable and complete before we reach them. Someday, we might realize just how sweet the seasons we're living in are—before the dream. The good old days.

As life passes on, and we step into one dream after another, we might look back and recognize the value of a season. At the same time, we can still appreciate that the Lord knew what He was talking about when He didn't intend for us to be alone. We may find that, despite how valuable independence is, we are better together. We were created to be with other people. Whether that looks like sweet friends for now or your person or both, *with* is a sweet place to be.

Together doesn't influence our value or purpose. Those things remain despite our status. Let's pursue our purpose in full force and welcome the people in our lives to propel our purpose together. Dreams are a good thing, especially if we use our faith and Father to reach them.

Learning from Little Ones

We have a lot to learn from little ones. As much as we have to teach them with our wisdom and experience, they have a lot to teach us with eyes that haven't been conditioned the way ours have.

My sister-in-law kept a picture of herself as a child on her desk to remember who she was then and to make that Alison proud. I loved that concept. Every day, we are becoming, and it's up to us who we become. Let's not leave behind the sweet and integral qualities that have and always will make up the cells of who we are.

A few chapters ago, we talked about four-year-old you and the process of becoming. Let's circle back to this concept and take it one step further. Let's say there was some way to time travel and be two places at once—and four-year-old you got to meet current-day you.

Are you who you thought you'd be? Would four-year-old you run up and hug your knees and look up at current-day you beaming with pride and excitement about who you are? Would four-year-old you peek out from the doorway and stand with a bit of hesitation, unfamiliar with who you've become?

Maybe you're different than you thought you'd be.

Maybe you're more than you thought you'd be.

Maybe not—but you're not done yet.

Take it all back to before everything happened, before you were taught to carry the weight of the world on your shoulders, and before the world kept asking and emphasizing the *what* instead of the *who*. What if you could share some wisdom with little you? What would you say to smooth out the road between four-year-old you and current-day you? And what advice would four-year-old you give to current-day you?

We're called to be like little children: innocent, pure, joyful, hopeful, present, excited, awed, and enchanted by the little things as much as the big things. Let's remember those things and hold onto that spirit.

The who we're becoming matters way more than the what. It always will. All of these perspectives and foresight are just reminders to sift through this life and hold on to what matters and let go of the rest. We don't give little ones enough credit for recognizing the things that matter.

The what of our lives may stack our resumes and our bank accounts for a number of years, but the who will decide our forever.

I think we have a whole lot to learn from our four-year-old selves, fresh from our heavenly Father's arms. You've got a whole lot of your life left—let's start right here. See if you can find a picture of yourself as a little one. Maybe it will inspire you in your day-to-day life to make four-year-old you proud of who you are and who you are becoming. Let's remember who we were then and use that spirit to propel our purpose and multiply our impact.

Chapter 27

IT'S OK

BELLY SLIDES IN THE BOARDROOM ARE A FUN CHILDHOOD MEMORY. I went to a birthday party that looked much different than most. It was at an alumni building at a university. Somehow, as nine-year-olds, we ended up spending most of the party in the boardroom. Why not? We slid on our bellies across the long wooden boardroom tables and played tag on both sides of it.

If only boardrooms were that much fun today. All my current experiences in boardrooms look much different. I think that birthday party was so memorable because that experience took a boardroom out of context. My affiliation with boardrooms and boredom was uprooted and replaced with fun. It wasn't what I thought it was supposed to be.

It's OK when things look different than how you thought they would. That might be a good thing. The Lord may allow seasons to look different than you thought they were supposed to in order to uproot your expectations and make room for His reality. Let down your guard to things being different than you thought they would be. God may be taking it out of context to replace our perceptions with something that is way better. That childhood memory disarms the intimidation of a boardroom, and now I always walk in with a reflective smile and little chuckle, wondering if I should give it another belly slide for old times' sake.

DIFFERENT

In some seasons, things are different than we thought they would be in a challenging way. In some seasons, the differences are hard. Hold tight to the purpose you have in that place because that season of life is still worth living well.

It's OK if this season looks different than you thought it would.

It's OK if things look, feel, sound, smell, and taste different than you thought they would.

It's OK if they're different from what they once were.

It's OK if you come home to an empty house these days and set a table for one.

It's OK if you come home to an overwhelming, well-lived-in home that you can't seem to keep up with.

It's OK if you thought things would be different by now.

It's OK if "having it all together" looks different than you imagined.

It's OK if things are different.

It's OK if the differences are still uncomfortable. Different is OK.

We can let down our guard to the unfamiliarity it may bring. We are capable of handling new, unfamiliar, and different. Breath by breath, the unfamiliar will become more and more familiar. The cold space will soon warm up. This place will soon become a new territory of who you are. New grounds will mark the growth you have traversed in this season. They are expanding who you are and who you are becoming. There's still good here. There's still hope here. In all our seasons, we have to search and fight for the good things. We need to see them and recognize them. This remains true at this point in time too. Maybe you have to look a little closer or fight a little harder for them, but they're still here. Give yourself grace. You're learning.

All that is different—and continues to show up different—will propel growth. New things are coming. The Lord is still working.

Even here, there is air to breathe and space to grow. It's OK if this season looks different than you thought it would. This is a terrain you're learning to traverse.

Expectations versus Reality

Differences can come in many shapes, sizes, and degrees. Maybe the recipe tasted different than you thought it would, maybe your pants fit differently than you thought they would, maybe a conversation went differently than you thought it would, or maybe your day went differently than you thought it would. It's funny how we formulate expectations based on what we think something has been or is supposed to be. Differences are counted as the things that deviate from our expectations. It's in our nature to wake up and think through what we have in the day and the schedule of events. We might even develop subconscious expectations for the day ahead. We might try to bring our own agendas into an unpredictable world, which makes change an inevitable factor.

Let's embrace that and make the place of unexpected change our wheelhouse, the space where we thrive. Let's not bat an eye when things go differently than how we thought they would and roll with it and make the most of how it plays out. Different isn't a downgrade or a disruption. The Lord knew how things would go all along. We can trust the One who is in control. He is good.

Chapter 28

FIND THE LESSON

As we come across the twists and turns, remember that there's a lesson to be learned in every story. Growth is a continuous opportunity we will find when we look for it. Let's search for it. Our ability to find the lesson and take on the posture of a learner of life enables us to continually grow. A posture of learning teaches us to press in on our purpose. It carves a place for peace in the midst of the twists and turns where there once was none.

Writing this book looked much different than I thought it would. I wrote this book in a season where words escaped me. Writing had always been my most natural state, but it had diminished in some way. I believed it was the Lord's intention for my life at the time. It required me to lean on the Lord, word by word, and he showed up. I found so much power and peace by relying on God's abilities instead of my own.

Let's welcome the differences as situations and seasons that expand our comfort zones and refine our attitudes and aptitudes. Differences are the evidence of changing seasons and growth; they are natural rhythms of life.

Let down your guard to natural rhythms. If you are up against all the waves of uncertainty, don't resist. Don't try to unpack and understand every bit—as tempting as it might be. Just focus on each breath, let each wave come as it will, and ride it out. Let it take you up and back down and up and back down. The One who holds authority over the wind and waves is in the thick of it with you. He is making a way where there is no way. That's just who He is. And through it all, He is refining you and carrying you closer to His shores.

Let's let our guard down to differences. It may be uprooting something good for something better or just be proof of the changing seasons. All of that is refining you and propelling your purpose.

DISCERNING THE ROUTE

As we face countless changes and rattles to our expectations day after day, let's learn from the One who understands. Jesus held onto what was steady despite every bump and turn in the road. He knew the route because He knew His destination. Since He knew where the winding road would lead Him, He was faithful throughout the journey. Jesus knew everything along the route was part of the plan, and He was postured to impact by His purpose and power.

When we're after the will of God through His Word, everything along the path home is part of the plan and ready for our impact by the purpose we've been given. Jesus was able to discern the roads that were meant to be traveled alone, despite their weight and loneliness. He knew the road to Golgotha was intended to be traveled alone so no one else in the world would ever have to do it again. There were also moments when He gathered with people. Jesus knew when to gather and when to separate.

There are times when moments with our heavenly Father are what we need. It's where we'll find fuel for our purpose and a refill of peace. Other times, there is holiness in gathering. Prayer is our best method of discernment. Remember how often Jesus went up to the mountainside to pray, going somewhere to just be with His Father.

Jesus was faithful with what He had—no matter how little. Whether that meant showing up or noticing a need, He was faithful.

Regardless of His circumstances, He was not distracted by what He didn't have. Jesus knew He didn't need anything but His Father to do what He was sent to accomplish. It's the same for us. We have everything we need in our Father to do what He has sent us to do. He has equipped us to accomplish what He has in mind.

Despite every difference we face and every rattled expectation, everything we have is a gift we've been entrusted to care for. Let's be good stewards of them. Whether they are our purpose, our bodies, our opportunities, our spaces, our families, or everything in between, we have a whole bunch to learn from our Savior and King. He's the most faithful and gracious Teacher. Let's be faithful with the little things, believing it all carries more than what we can see in our purpose and peace.

Chapter 29
Captivated by Purpose

When I lived in Ohio, I loved visiting the garden center. The huge greenhouse was overflowing with the most beautiful plants. There were countless plants of all types. I don't know much about plants, but there were water plants, succulents, large plants, small plants, weird plants, and cute plants. I loved visiting and moseying through the aisles, fully immersed in all the beauty. It was such a peaceful oasis. I loved the gentle sound of running water and the beauty of everything blooming. It's amazing how well they take care of every plant. The owners say the key is light, consistent watering, and pruning. Light is needed for energy, water is needed for growth, and pruning makes room for new growth and allows the plant's energy to go where it's needed.

Pruning is an interesting concept. It's something we need too. Every season welcomes a check of our life's inventory: a look at what's steady and good, what's old and expired, and what's new. Some things are meant to be tossed out or just moved on from. Some things can stick around, and some things are making their debut.

Everything blooms at its own pace. Plants take up the space they need to grow. They sprawl out when they need to. They reach tall, they reach wide, they reach deep, and they don't apologize for it. Every bit of space is counted as beautiful and wanted. If one plant is blooming tall, wide, and deep, and its neighboring plant is in a much different state, it's just in a different season. The differences between the two—one tall and blooming and one just barely budding—don't influence how they grow. They're not comparing their statuses in different seasons. They are each taking up the space and time they need to grow without being distracted by comparison. They are so captivated by their purpose that they aren't distracted by where they measure up. A season of pruning may not look as pretty as a season of blooming, but the seasons will ebb and flow. Each and every season is valued equally and purposed differently.

We'll face seasons of budding and blooming too. Some seasons will have painful pruning or easy growth. We can trust that both are valuable seasons because our heavenly Father is the Gardner. His hand is so careful with you. He works everything for good, and He is refining you to be more like His Son. He will do what's good in His eyes, which is what's best. Let's be so captivated by purpose that we aren't distracted by where we measure up. All creation points to the Creator. That's how He intended it. Let's learn from plants a bit more. They point toward our heavenly Father. Regardless of the season you're in, whether budding or blooming, there is purpose where you are. Look for it.

THE MALIBU ZIP LINE

My favorite kind of tree is an evergreen. Young Life's Malibu Club is lined with evergreens. While I was there, there were forest fires in the Pacific Northwest, and the smoke drifted all the way to British Columbia. For days on end, the smoke would nestle on top of the trees and cover them. The smoke was thick enough that we couldn't even see the panorama of mountains surrounding the camp. Each day, camp would wake up eager to see if the smoke had lifted. We were all eager to see what we knew existed behind the veil of smoke.

What if we woke up each day with this same eager anticipation to see the Lord in everything. What if we woke up eager to follow the trace of His hand and holy work. The veil will be lifted someday.

Another similar way I saw the Lord at Malibu was the fog. The fog loved to trinkle down the mountaintops and rest on the trees. We often couldn't see the trees because they were engulfed by the fog. If we did, it was just a silhouette peeking through translucent fog. Imagine we are the trees, and the fog is the Holy Spirit. When we're so engulfed by the Holy Spirit, all people see of us is Jesus. I want to be like the Malibu trees where the fog rested on them. I want the Holy Spirit to rest on me so much that it's all anyone sees—all anyone sees of me is Jesus.

I got to witness the beauty of the resting fog while up in the trees as an intern. I helped run the zip line canopy tour. The zip line weaved through the tall, beautiful, moss-covered British Columbian trees. My role included helping campers get their gear on, explaining the instructions and what to expect, and actually putting individuals on the zip line. I traveled to North Carolina for a special training and exams to be certified on the zip line, a ropes course, and a tree swing.

A few months after the training, I was at Malibu. After a few days to refresh training, I had my first group of campers up with me on the zip line. I was so nervous. I knew the campers trusted me to get them on and through the zip line safely. I was in charge of attaching each human to the cable, doing the final check to ensure they were safe, and releasing them from the platform to go down the zip line. I was responsible for their safety. With every individual, I went through the steps I had so carefully trained for and practiced. I never skipped one step. That was what I was there to do. That was my purpose in that role. Doubt only crept in when I questioned my purpose there—the purpose I had been trained and equipped to fulfill. Every camper got through the zip line safe and sound—most of the time with a huge, ear-to-ear smile.

By the end of the summer, my team and I had put thousands of individuals through the zip line. Within the first few weeks, it was second nature. I was confident I could keep them safe. I think it can be the same in our daily lives. Doubt creeps in when we question our purpose. Let's be so captivated by purpose that we aren't distracted or deceived by doubt.

WHEN THE WEIGHT HITS

I experienced doubt face-to-face during the marathon. I felt great through most of the 26.2 miles, but I bonked hard in the high teens. I'd never wanted to stop running so much in my life. I just wanted to stop. I just wanted to rest. My main goal going into the marathon was to run the entire marathon. In those high-teen miles, I was desperate. I just wanted to fall or collapse or throw up because all those things would allow me to stop. None of those things happened. Doubt was staring me down. For a while, I was believing its lies and letting it get to me.

I look back at that experience as one of my favorites. The marathon I was supposed to run was canceled about a month before race day. My version of the race was completely reimagined. My sweet family mapped out 26.2 miles along a bike path, and that became my new racecourse. They even rode their bikes on some of the course beforehand to be sure it would work. Although it was completely different from what I had imagined that day would look like, it was the best it could have ever been. I had all my closest people right beside me every mile. They biked the entire marathon. Their presence played an integral role. They could see when I was eye to eye with doubt, and could hear the weight of my feet getting heavier with every lie I believed. And with every lie, they spoke truth. They kept reminding me of my purpose there. They kept reminding me that I was created to do hard things. They reminded me that every step, no matter how heavy and hard, was progress in fulfilling my purpose there.

That reimagined marathon was such a sweet look at life. It showed me the power of community; no matter who that is or how many there are, there is power in people. We weren't created to run the race marked out before us alone. My closest people could be with me every step of the 26.2 miles. Regardless how close they were or how kind their words and care were, they couldn't do it for me. They couldn't take away the pain and discomfort. They couldn't get to the finish line for me. They couldn't face the doubt for me. It was just my two feet. In the thick of it, they were there. When I shared my hurt with them, they shared hope. When I was distracted by pain, they reminded me of my purpose. They kept reminding me to press on and practice my posture of praise in the pain. They continually encouraged me to recognize the power in persevering and pursuing peace in that place—exactly where and as I was. The people beside me remembered the good when I couldn't. They reminded me why I was there and why I was capable. They couldn't do it for me, but they told me why I could in the moments I didn't believe I was able.

Life is a lot like running a marathon. No one can run the race marked out for you. No one can take away the pain and discomfort. No one can get to the finish line for you. No one can face the doubt for you. It's just your two feet. In the thick of it, your people will be there. When you share hurt, they will share hope. When you're distracted by pain, they will remind you of your purpose. They'll encourage you to press on and practice a posture of praise in the pain. They will challenge you to recognize the power in persevering and pursuing peace in that place, exactly where and as you are.

People help us remember the good when we can't. They remind us that we're capable when we forget. They can't do a single step for you, but they will remind you why you can. This is the value of people. They challenge and encourage you to be captivated by purpose rather than distracted by doubt. They remind you of the peace where you are when you can't find it. The race marked before you is one the Lord has specifically created to refine you into the image of His Son and propel you toward your unique purpose. You've been created and equipped to do difficult things. No one can do it *for* you, but they can do it *with* you. You were created to run the race He set out for you.

Chapter 30

PEACE IN PURPOSE

PEACE IS FOUND IN THE SWEET SPOT OF OUR PURPOSE. EVERY season and story of your life plays into your purpose, and in every season and story, there is peace to be found. As we find peace in unexpected places, we'll find peace beginning to take up more and more space in who we are, slowly becoming something we carry into every situation. There is always peace to be realized. Let's never stop looking for it—even when it requires diving deep.

I love the look of marquee signs when every letter is filled with light bulbs. Imagine our names as a lit-up marquee sign. Our natural tendency is to wake up with the intention to add light bulbs to our names. What if we woke up with the intention of adding a light bulb to the name of Jesus. At the end of each day, let's think about whether we added a light bulb to our names or the name of Jesus. What good does it do for your name to be in lights? What good does that do for others? Let's bring light each and every day to the name that can save people. His name changes everything.

If you're still navigating your purpose, no worries; I am too. We always will be. Here's a clue we can hold onto along the way: our purpose has everything to do with adding a light bulb to the name of Jesus each and every day. Use your specific talents and abilities that the Lord created and predestined you with in order to carry out the eternal assignment He has entrusted you to accomplish.

You are strong. You are capable. You are worthy. You are chosen. You are seen. You are enough. You are valued. You are needed. You are holy and dearly loved. You are intentionally created. You are wisely woven together. You are eternally equipped. You are who you are on purpose and for a purpose. You are the King's kid, locked and loaded with power by a Savior who died to know you. Because of this Savior, Jesus Christ, we are able to remember the good and all the peace to be found in every season and story. And when we look for it, in the depths of darkness, in corners of confusion, and in peaks of purpose, we will find peace in all the unexpected places. And when we do, we'll find that, even here, it's OK.

04164360-00961165

Printed in the United States
by Baker & Taylor Publisher Services